WINNING
TURKEY

WINNING TURKEY

How America, Europe, and Turkey Can Revive a Fading Partnership

PHILIP H. GORDON

OMER TASPINAR

BROOKINGS INSTITUTION PRESS

Washington, D.C.

Copyright © 2008
THE BROOKINGS INSTITUTION
1775 Massachusetts Avenue, N.W., Washington, DC 20036.
www.brookings.edu

All rights reserved. No part of this publication may be reproduced or
transmitted in any form or by any means without permission in writing
from the Brookings Institution Press.

Library of Congress Cataloging-in-Publication data
Gordon, Philip H., 1962–
    Winning Turkey : how America, Europe, and Turkey can revive a fading
partnership / Philip Gordon and Omer Taspinar.
        p.   cm.
    Includes bibliographical references and index.
    Summary: "Explains current situation and designs a plan to ease tensions in
Turkey. Proposes a 'grand bargain' between Turkey and the Kurds, advocating
greater support for increased liberalism and democracy, renewed European and
Turkish commitment to promote EU membership, a historic compromise with
Armenia, and greater Western engagement with Turkish Cypriots"—Provided by
publisher.
    ISBN 978-0-8157-3215-0 (pbk. : alk. paper)
    1. Minorities—Government policy—Turkey   2. Islam and politics—Turkey
3. Turkey—Politics and government—1980–   4. Turkey—Ethnic relations
5. European Union—Turkey.   6. United States—Foreign relations—Turkey.
7. Turkey—Foreign relations—United States.   I. Taspinar, Omer, 1970–
II. Title.
    JQ1803.5.M5G67 2008
    327.561—dc22   2008030573

9 8 7 6 5 4 3 2 1

The paper used in this publication meets minimum requirements of the
American National Standard for Information Sciences—Permanence of Paper
for Printed Library Materials: ANSI Z39.48-1992.

Typeset in Minion

Composition by R. Lynn Rivenbark
Macon, Georgia

Printed by R. R. Donnelley
Harrisonburg, Virginia

Contents

Acknowledgments

THE AUTHORS ARE grateful to the Brookings Institution for its generous support of the research that provided the basis for this work, which included several trips to Turkey for interviews. Parts of chapter 2 appeared previously in Omer Taspinar's "The Old Turks Revolt," *Foreign Affairs* (November–December 2007), pp. 114–30. The authors are also grateful to Henri Barkey, Cengiz Candar, Allison Hart, Michael Leigh, Soli Ozel, Mark Parris, Carlos Pascual, and Jeremy Shapiro for their comments on an earlier draft.

CHAPTER ONE

Introduction:
Who Lost Turkey?

IMAGINE THE FOLLOWING scene at a possible presidential debate focusing on foreign policy, in the late fall of 2012. The moderator, Jim Lehrer, poses the question:

> For over fifty years, the Republic of Turkey was a staunch American ally and important partner in the Middle East. But over the past several years it has decisively distanced itself from the West. A few years ago the Turkish military overthrew the elected Islamist-leaning government, which it accused of promoting a hidden Islamic fundamentalist agenda and selling out Turkey's national interests. In response to U.S. and European sanctions, the new military regime angrily declared that it would pursue a more independent foreign policy. It withdrew its application to join the European Union, suspended its membership in NATO, and barred the United States from using military bases in Turkey to transit equipment to Iraq. It has developed closer diplomatic, economic, and energy relations with Russia, China, and Iran, and has sent Turkish forces into northern

Iraq to act against the Kurds. How could the United States let this happen to our relationship with such an important American ally? As president what would you have done to prevent this foreign policy disaster? Who lost Turkey? And how can we win it back?

Of course, such a scenario may not take place in 2012—or ever, for that matter. But anyone who dismisses such a possibility has not been paying attention, and anybody not thinking now about how to avoid such a scenario risks failing to do what is necessary to prevent it. Indeed, a series of major political and strategic factors are now converging to raise questions about the future of Turkey's long-standing Western and democratic orientation. Turkey's relationship with the United States is deeply strained, and anti-Americanism has surged; one 2008 poll showed that Turkey had the least positive view of the United States of any country in the world.[1] Turkey's hopes of joining the European Union, which were high as recently as the EU's October 2005 decision to begin accession negotiations, have also been deflated—a majority of Turks now doubt whether Turkey will ever get in. Add to the mix a Turkish society deeply polarized along secular and religious lines, the revival of terrorist attacks by the separatist Kurdish Workers' Party (Partiya Karkeren Kurdistan—PKK), growing Western support for official recognition that the Turks perpetrated a genocide against the Armenians in the early twentieth century, and deep resentment in Turkey that the West has not delivered on its promise to ease the isolation of the Turkish Cypriots and you have the makings of a severe Turkish backlash against the West.

Given Turkey's overwhelmingly Muslim population and consecutive election victories by a political party with Islamic roots, many equate the notion of "losing Turkey" with the idea of an Islamic revival. In fact, however, although the growing importance of religion in Turkey is having a major impact on Turkish society, the threat to Turkey's Western orientation today is not so much Islamization but growing nationalism and frustration with the United States and Europe. A majority of Turks still want to see their country firmly anchored in the West, but their patience is wearing thin because of what they perceive to be Western double standards and neglect of Turkish national security interests.

Furthermore, in an ironic twist, the principal challenge to Turkey's Western orientation is coming not from Islamist politicians but from the secularist establishment that has long had close ties to the West. Turkey's Kemalist establishment (named for Mustafa Kemal Ataturk, the founder of modern Turkey) and its supporters believe the government of the Justice and Development Party (Adalet ve Kalkinma Partisi—AKP) under Prime Minister Recep Tayyip Erdogan is pursuing a hidden Islamic agenda and blame the United States and Europe for supporting it. The degree of alarm among Turkish secularists is underestimated by foreign observers, who tend to see "moderate Islam" as a positive alternative to Muslim fundamentalism—an alternative to the "clash of civilizations"—in the post-9/11 world. Yet Western praise of Turkey as a "moderate Islamic country" only exacerbates the fears and concerns of Turkish secularists, who do not want their country to be an experiment in "moderate Islamization." The Kemalists also believe the AKP government is too soft on Kurdish separatists, again pursuing a dangerous policy encouraged and abetted by the United States. In other words, concerning the two greatest perceived threats to Turkey in the eyes of the Kemalist establishment—Islamism and the Kurdish question— the AKP and the West are seen to be on the wrong side. These dynamics have already created a chasm between Kemalism and the West. And they have realigned the traditional foreign policy orientations of Turkey's major domestic groups: the once Eastern-oriented Islamists are now the ones more interested in maintaining close ties with Europe and the United States, whereas the once Western-oriented Kemalist elites are questioning the value of close Turkish ties with the West.

In the past, Americans and Europeans would often ask whether Turkey had any realistic geopolitical alternatives to allying itself with the West and complacently reassured themselves that it did not. But today such alternatives are starting to look more realistic to many Turks. If the strategic relationship with the United States continues to erode and prospects for joining the EU continue to recede, Turkey could opt for a more nationalistic and authoritarian path, perhaps combining a version of isolationism with closer relations with sometime rivals of the United States such as Russia, Iran, China, and Syria. Americans and Europeans who do not take the risk of such a development seriously underestimate the degree of resentment of the West that has been building up in the country.

Turkish politicians and officials, it should be made clear— including the current Justice and Development Party (AKP) government under Prime Minister Recep Tayyip Erdogan—are committed to maintaining Turkey's Western and democratic orientation. In early 2008, moreover, Turkish feelings about the United States improved, at least temporarily, following Washington's agreement to support Turkish military action against the PKK in Iraq. At the same time, however, both external and internal factors are still pushing Turkey in the opposite direction. Ongoing uncertainty about the war in Iraq, increased Kurdish terrorism, new obstacles to EU accession, and developments in Cyprus and Armenia are leading some Turks to question the value of their long-standing geopolitical alignments. Domestically, the intense polarization between the AKP and the secularist establishment does not bode well for Turkish democracy.

The stakes for the United States and Europe in Turkey's future are high. Home to more than 70 million Muslims, Turkey is, for all its problems, the most advanced democracy in the Islamic world. It has borders with Armenia, Azerbaijan, Bulgaria, Georgia, Greece, Iran, Iraq, and Syria. It has a rapidly growing economy and an annual GDP of nearly $700 billion, making it one of the twenty largest economies in the world. It is the corridor through which the vast energy reserves of the Caspian Sea and Central Asia will pass to the West—the only alternative being Iran. A stable, Western-oriented, liberal Turkey on a clear path toward EU membership would serve as a growing market for Western goods, a contributor of the labor forces Europe will desperately need, a democratic example for the rest of the Muslim world, a stabilizing influence on Iraq, a partner in Afghanistan, and a critical ally in the war on terrorism—not a bad list of attributes. A resentful, unstable, and inward-looking Turkey, on the other hand, would be the opposite in every case; if its domestic politics went wrong it could not only cease being a close friend but could become an actual adversary of the West. None of this means that the United States or its European allies should craft their policies on the sole basis of satisfying Turkish nationalism; Turkey is a difficult and sometimes insecure partner whose demands are often hard to satisfy. It does, however, mean that it would be folly to ignore the consequences of actions that have such an important impact on this strategically critical state.

Given these stakes and implications, Western leaders should be doing all they can so that we do not need to have a debate—in four years, or ever—about "who lost Turkey." To that end, leaders in the United States, Europe, and Turkey should be asking themselves what they could do now to avoid the scenario outlined earlier. We propose five main steps:

—Promotion of a "grand bargain" between Turkey and the Kurds

—Western support for liberalism and democracy in Turkey

—A renewed commitment by the European Union and Turkey to support eventual Turkish membership

—Promotion of a historic compromise with Armenia

—Support for a political settlement in Cyprus and greater Western engagement with Turkish Cypriots

Such achievable steps (fleshed out in the final chapter) are not only worthy goals on their own merits, but they could also go a long way toward preventing an unnecessary, damaging, and potentially permanent split between Turkey and the West. Turkey need not be "lost" to the West, but it will be, unless there is concerted action from the United States, Europe, and, most important, Turkey itself.

CHAPTER TWO

Kemalists, Islamists, and the West

COUNTRIES SEEKING MEMBERSHIP in the European Union do not usually come to the brink of a military coup. Yet that is precisely where Turkey found itself on April 27, 2007, after weeks of mounting tensions between the country's generals and the AKP.

The AKP, a conservative populist party with Islamic roots, had announced its decision to nominate Foreign Minister Abdullah Gul, a well-respected politician and the architect of the party's ambitious drive to get Turkey into the EU, to the prestigious post of president.[1] The media and the business community welcomed the choice as a conciliatory sign; they were relieved that Recep Tayyip Erdogan—the more controversial prime minister who had once been convicted for inciting religious hatred because he had recited a poem with Islamic undertones—would not be running. But the fervently secularist military and the Republican People's Party (Cumhuriyet Halk Partisi—CHP), a center-left nationalist opposition party, were unhappy. To them, the presidency was the last bastion of secularism, and Gul, who once flirted with political Islam and whose wife wears a headscarf, posed an existential threat to the republic.

The CHP, along with other parties, boycotted the first round of the election in parliament on April 27, and the vote proved inconclusive—Gul failed to get the two-thirds majority required of a presidential candidate in the first two rounds of voting. There was little doubt that the AKP would eventually prevail, however, since in a third round, if it came to that, a simple majority would do. But that day, the CHP also challenged the whole process before the Constitutional Court, asking that the election be annulled on the dubious grounds that a presidential candidate needed not just two-thirds of votes actually cast in parliament but a quorum of two-thirds of the all the members of parliament, whether they voted or not. That night, all eyes were on the court.

Just as television pundits were debating how long it would take for the Constitutional Court to issue a decision, the military got involved. Shortly before midnight an announcement was posted on the Turkish General Staff's official website alleging that "certain circles . . . are waging a relentless struggle to erode the founding principles of the Turkish Republic, starting with secularism." The military went on to warn, "If necessary, the Turkish Armed Forces will not hesitate to make their position . . . abundantly clear as the absolute defenders of secularism." Given Turkey's history of military interventions, the memorandum—dubbed an "e-coup" by the press—was a thinly veiled threat that a more conventional coup might be in the offing.

Many expected that Prime Minister Erdogan, faced with such a risk, would compromise and opt for a presidential candidate acceptable to the secularist establishment. Instead, the AKP condemned the military's attempt to influence the judiciary and maintained Gul's candidacy. A few days later, breaking with precedents including Turgut Ozal's presidential election in 1989, the Constitutional Court decided that parliament lacked the necessary quorum for a valid presidential election. With parliament now unable to select anyone at all, the government called early general elections for July 22. A coup was thus avoided, and a semblance of democracy maintained.

Turkey was on edge during the following three months. Political polarization over the country's deeply rooted identity problems worsened amid concerns that the military might once again step in. Millions took to the streets in anti-AKP demonstrations, some orchestrated by retired generals. But Prime Minister Erdogan held his ground and asked the Turkish people to consider his political and economic record rather than the sinister scenarios of creeping Islamization put forward by his opponents. The thwarted presidential candidate Gul specifically denied any "hidden agenda," calling on voters to "look at what we have done in government for four and a half years. We have worked harder than any party in Turkey's history to make this country a member of the European Union. We have passed hundreds of laws that have freed up the economy and strengthened human rights. Why would we do this if we were trying to Islamize Turkey?"[2] Under the AKP, Turkey's per capita income had doubled, its democratic record had improved significantly, and it had begun accession negotiations with the EU.

In the end, the AKP won a landslide victory in the July 2007 elections. It won 47 percent of the vote, up from 34 percent in 2002, and more than twice as many votes as any other party. This outcome was less a victory of Islam over secularism than a victory for the new democratic, pro-market, and globally integrated Turkey over the old authoritarian, statist, and introverted one. As many Turkish journalists put it, the July 22 elections represented "the people's memorandum"—a rebuke to the generals' online memorandum of April 27. The electoral performance of the AKP exceeded all expectations. Turnout was a record 88 percent, with millions of Turks cutting short their holidays to cast ballots. The

AKP secured 341 of the 550 seats in the parliament, enough to once again form a government on its own, but short of the two-thirds needed to force through its choice of president. The CHP came in second, with only 21 percent of the vote and 112 seats, and the right-wing Nationalist Action Party (Milliyetci Haraket Partisi—MHP) received 14 percent and 71 seats. Some twenty-seven independents, most of them from the pro-Kurdish Democratic Society Party (Demokratik Toplum Partisi—DTP), made it into parliament as well.

In August, the AKP-dominated parliament crowned its victory by electing Abdullah Gul to the presidency with the support of the MHP. Gul sought to ease the fears of his critics by declaring that he would abide by the secular principles of the republic and continue to steer Turkey toward the EU. But the secularists remain unconvinced. Turkey's top military leadership boycotted Gul's inauguration and refused to salute the new president during his first official engagement. Even more seriously, in March 2008 the chief prosecutor of Turkey's Supreme Court of Appeals called for the disbanding of the AKP on the grounds of "antisecular activities." The indictment was a response to the government's proposed constitutional amendments aimed at lifting the ban on headscarves in universities, an important symbol of Turkey's secular orientation.

In a 162-page indictment, Chief Prosecutor Abdurrahman Yalcinkaya argued that the AKP was using democracy as a vehicle for imposing a religious political system and asked the Constitutional Court to apply a five-year ban on more than seventy AKP officials, including Erdogan and Gul. In his indictment, Yalcinkaya cited evidence—mostly speeches by party members—going back to the party's foundation in 2001. The indictment reflected Kemalist concerns not only about Islam but about the West, noting that the AKP had "the support of forces behind globalization" and that "Turkey has become the co-sponsor of the Greater Middle East project which promotes the ideology of 'moderate Islam.'"[3] The trigger for the indictment may have been the AKP's controversial move to lift the headscarf ban in universities, but Yalcinkaya's primary target seems to have been Erdogan himself. The indictment cites sixty-one different pieces of evidence—more than for any other of the seventy-one people accused—that it claims demonstrate Erdogan's attempts to undermine secularism.[4] Most of these statements were made after the AKP first took office in November 2002. However, speeches by Erdogan in the mid-1990s, when he was a member of the Welfare Party (Refah Partisi—RP), are also included.

On July 31, 2008, the Constitutional Court, the same one that sought to block Gul's election in the first place, ruled by a vote of 10 to 1 that the AKP was indeed guilty of violating the country's secular principles, and penalized it by cutting the party's public financing in half. Six of the judges voted for a penalty of outright closure of the party, just one short of the seven required for that measure to pass. A major crisis was thus averted, but the warning to the AKP about future activities was clear.

The Pillars of Kemalism

The Turkish military and secular establishment's concern about the "Islamist threat" dates back to the foundation of the Turkish Republic, when Mustafa Kemal, known as Ataturk, promoted an ideology that remains powerful in Turkey today. Ataturk is the legendary founder of modern Turkey. His immense popularity stems primarily from his having saved Turkey from foreign occupation and subjugation after the breakup of the Ottoman Empire at the end of World War I. Turkey's independence, sense of national pride, dignity, and sovereignty are all directly associated with Ataturk.

Ataturk's ideology, known as "Kemalism," had three main pillars, the first of which was radical secularism. The Kemalists' "civilizing mission" was influenced by the ideals of the French Revolution and especially the French anticlerical tradition of *laïcité*, a particularly militant form of state-enforced secularism. In both France and Turkey, religion became a symbol of the *ancien régime* and opposition to the republic. Fervently committed to assuming progressive roles against reactionary enemies, the proponents of both French *laïcité* and its Kemalist analogue, *laiklik*, were keen on taking religion out of the public sphere. For them, *laiklik* was the dividing line between enlightened and obscurantist, progressive and conservative, modern and traditional.

Turkish secularism readily grafted itself onto a long-standing tradition of state hegemony over religion, a legacy of the Ottoman Empire. Ottoman sultans had often enacted laws outside the realm of Islamic sharia, on the basis of political rather than religious principles. When Islam and the Ottoman Empire's political and national interests clashed, the sultans favored the state. Similarly, the Kemalists maintained firm control over the Islamic establishment and the religious class of *ulema* (Islamic legal scholars) because they saw religion as a political threat and Islam, in particular, as a cause of social, cultural, political, and economic decline. Having realized, however, that eradicating Islam altogether was not a realistic option, they tried to promote a "civilized" version of it. Instead of formally separating state and religion (as France did in 1905), modern Turkey monopolized religious functions and incorporated religious personnel into the state bureaucracy in order to better control religion. To this day, the government-controlled Directorate of Religious Affairs supervises and regulates Islam throughout Turkey, appoints and pays the country's imams, and issues standardized sermons to be read out in thousands of mosques each Friday.

The second pillar of Kemalism was assimilationist nationalism. Modern Turkey actively sought to assimilate all of its Muslim minorities. "Turkishness" came to be defined as a common national, linguistic, and territorial identity, superseding tribal and other ethnic identities. Again taking France as its model, the Kemalist regime rejected the concept of multiculturalism; no communal structure would stand between the republic and its citizens. Unlike the Ottoman elites, the Kemalists rejected multi-ethnic and multinational cosmopolitanism. The new Turkish Republic recognized non-Muslims as Turkish citizens but engaged in de facto discrimination against them, banning Armenians, Greeks, and Jews from holding government jobs. Thus, ironically, the "secular" Turkish republic turned out to be less tolerant toward its non-Muslim minorities than the "Islamic" Ottoman Empire had been, partly because "Turkishness" was still associated with being Muslim.

Predictably, assimilationist nationalism and militant secularism faced violent resistance and opposition from ethnic Kurds and proponents of Islamic rule, especially in the semiautonomous Kurdish provinces of southeastern Turkey, which had had little exposure to centralization, state structures, and nation building during Ottoman times. In fact, Kemalist supremacy was finally established only after the military suppressed more than a dozen Kurdish Islamic uprisings in the 1920s and 1930s. These major rebellions traumatized the young republic's military leaders and created their suspicion of all things Kurdish and Islamic, which endures to this day. They also reinforced the feeling that the new republic was and would remain vulnerable to breakup—a sentiment that had already taken root in the Western powers' attempts to carve up the Anatolian remains of the Ottoman Empire in the Treaty of Sèvres in 1920. Henceforth, the generals concluded, they would have to act as the resolute custodians of secularism and nationalism.

A third pillar of Kemalism was Ataturk's determination to transform the Republic of Turkey into a modern, Western country, anchored geopolitically to the West. Already in the waning years of the Ottoman Empire in the late nineteenth century, Istanbul launched one of the earliest Westernization projects in history. Having suffered a series of humiliating defeats at the hands of European armies and having grudgingly recognized the superiority of Western military technique, the Ottoman military was the first institution to modernize. Its troops adopted European weapons, and its academies, Western sciences and educational methods. Its top cadres became Europe's greatest emulators. Ataturk himself was a product of this movement in the military.

A more radical form of Westernization came on the eve of World War I under the Young Turks and after the war under the leadership of Ataturk. In the 1920s and 1930s, the Kemalists, mostly military men who had been exposed to Western-style positivist education in Ottoman military academies, adopted a top-down project of radical modernization for the new Turkey. Ataturk's models for Turkey were the advanced, industrialized, democratic nation-states of the West that had won the World War. If Turkey was to find its rightful place in the twentieth-century world—or merely survive without being carved up by the Great Powers, like the other Muslim lands in the Middle East—it would have to do so as part of the West.

In an ambitious drive to import European civilization, the republic abolished the caliphate and the use of the Arabic alphabet, Islamic education, and the Sufi brotherhoods. It adopted Western legal codes from Germany, Italy, and Switzerland, together with the Latin alphabet, the Western calendar, Western holidays, and Western measuring systems. The country's official history and language were reworked. A new education system glorified pre-Islamic Turkic civilizations at the expense of the country's more recent Ottoman (and Islamic) past, and many Arabic and Persian words were purged to create an "authentically" Turkish vocabulary. In the name of secularism, even the Islamic call to prayer was translated from Arabic into modern Turkish. Western clothing became the new compulsory dress code for men, and the traditional Ottoman headgear, known as a fez, was banned. Women were discouraged from wearing the Islamic veil.

Despite such ambitious reforms, however, Kemalist secularism barely infiltrated Turkish society at large. The rural and pious masses of Anatolia remained largely unaffected by Ankara's attempts at cultural reengineering. It was the military, the government bureaucracy, and the small urban bourgeoisie who adapted most readily to Kemalism's thorough Westernization. Winning hearts and minds in the countryside would have required the use of traditional and religious symbols, but those were anathema to the Turkish Republic's founding fathers. In short order, the cultural gap between the Kemalist center and the Anatolian periphery had become insurmountable. As a Republican People's Party (CHP) slogan from the 1920s put it, the Turkish government seemed to rule "For the People, Despite the People."

Turkey and the Cold War

After Ataturk's death, in 1938, Ismet Inonu, another military hero turned statesman, assumed the presidency. He kept Turkey out of World War II, but soon after the conflict ended the Soviet Union's territorial ambitions became clear, and Turkey urgently wanted to join the free world. Before long, Turkey had become NATO's southern bulwark against the Soviet Union, and its credentials as an ally of the West were undisputed. In a cold war world dominated by nuclear threats and a delicate balance of power, thorny questions concerning Turkey's military interventions, human rights standards, and Muslim identity were rarely raised. Turkey fell neatly into the bipolar configuration of the cold war; realpolitik dictated its inclusion in "the West."

On the other hand, the cold war also forced Turkey to enter the age of democracy. The prospect of joining NATO and qualifying for U.S. assistance under the Marshall Plan encouraged Inonu to hold multiparty elections. Furthermore, as communism emerged as the new major domestic threat, Kemalist secularism and nationalism slowly lost their political relevance. So did Islam and Kurdish nationalism, the twin threats of the 1930s, at least on the surface. The new fault line dividing Turkey seemed to be ideological—an opposition between right and left—rather than religious or ethnic. Kurdish and Muslim dissent did not fully vanish, of course, but it was transformed. Kurdish discontent was redefined in terms of a class struggle, and it found a home in Turkey's fledgling socialist movement; political Islam joined forces with conservative anti-communist political parties.

Despite democratization, one thing hardly changed during the cold war: Turkey remained politically unstable, and each time the Turkish General Staff (the top military command) thought the republic was in danger, it intervened. It ousted civilian governments three times during the cold war—in 1960, 1971, and 1980—on each occasion staying in power only long enough to restore law and order. The 1960 coup ousted the Democrat Party, a conservative movement representing the Anatolian periphery that had easily won all the free elections held between 1950 and 1960. The deposed prime minister, Adnan Menderes, was sentenced to death and executed for "subversion against the constitutional order." The interventions of 1971 and 1980 had strong antileftist tendencies, and that of 1980, in particular, brutally crushed Kurdish and leftist dissent, but only temporarily.

Kurdish nationalism and ethnic identity were ruthlessly opposed and denied for decades, but never entirely went away. Instances of torture and killings in the Diyarbakir military prison between 1980 and 1983 helped plant the seeds of Kurdish ethnic separatism in Turkey's southeastern region. In 1984 a formerly communist Kurdish movement with a strong regional following, the PKK, launched a separatist terrorist insurgency. The military rulers' method of mobilizing state-controlled Islam proved equally counterproductive. To counter and depoliticize the left-wing student population, the generals expanded the budget of the Directorate of Religious Affairs, increased the number of Islamic high schools throughout the country, and introduced compulsory courses on religion in primary and middle schools. In an attempt to create a united Turkish-Islamic front against communism, they also granted Muslim constituencies certain rights; for instance, they struck a law prohibiting graduates of Islamic high schools from studying subjects other than theology at universities. But by doing so, the military also inadvertently boosted the number of youths sympathetic to political Islam.

Islamism Versus Secularism after the Cold War

Especially after the death in 1993 of Turgut Ozal (prime minister, 1983–89; president, 1989–93), political instability seemed to become a permanent condition. Nine different coalition governments ruled Turkey in the 1990s alone. Such instability undermined the Turkish economy, which suffered throughout the postwar period from excessive state regulation, governmental corruption, and a rate of inflation that was so out of hand that eventually a cup of Turkish coffee was priced in the millions of Turkish lira.

During this period it seemed as if the Turkish Republic was back in the 1920s and 1930s, once again facing the twin challenges that had defined its founding years, political Islam and Kurdish dissent. And despite a radically different international context, Ankara's response took a classic Kemalist form: an authoritarian determination to reject any cultural or political compromise. The result was the "lost decade of the 1990s"—a decade of war with Kurdish separatists, polarization between secularists and Islamists, economic turmoil, and systemic corruption.

The Kurdish crisis was particularly badly timed in terms of Turkey's aspirations to become part of the West: it came just as Turkey needed to demonstrate its democratic credentials to the EU, which had seemed skeptical since Turkey first applied for membership in 1963. The Turkish military's conflict with the PKK cost the country dearly. Between 1984 and 1999, the internal struggle killed 40,000 people and consumed, in military expenditures alone, an estimated $120 billion (nearly the equivalent of Turkey's average annual GDP during this period). It seemed to quash all hope that the country might democratize soon. Also, to Ankara's dismay, many within the EU were sympathetic to the Kurds, seeing the conflict as the legitimate rebellion of an ethnic group whose cultural and political rights were being denied by an authoritarian regime.

In the meantime, the influence of the pro-Islamist Welfare Party rose, exacerbating the Kemalists' sense of insecurity. In 1994, at the height of both an acute financial crisis and the military struggle against Kurdish separatists, the Welfare Party shocked the secularist establishment by winning local elections nationwide and capturing control of Turkey's two largest metropolitan areas, Istanbul and Ankara: the capital would now be run by an Islamist mayor. Just a year later, another Welfare Party victory, this time in parliamentary elections, put an Islamist-led coalition in charge of the entire country.

The secularist establishment began to worry that the new Islamist-led government would adopt an overtly Islamic agenda and authoritarian manners. They feared it would suppress the secularist opposition, promote the wearing of Islamic headscarves, and challenge Turkey's alliances with Western states. In fact, notwithstanding their sometimes radical rhetoric, the Welfare Party and Prime Minister Necmettin Erbakan did not challenge the fundamental principles of Turkey's secular state. The party did try to plant its sympathizers in the ministries it controlled, but so had many previous governments. Still, the secularist press rang the alarm, warning of an imminent Islamist revolution. On February 28, 1997, the military, supported by civil-society organizations and the secularist press, forced Erbakan and his party out of power. Unlike previous military interventions, this one did not require any actual use of force (other than a symbolic display of tanks in a suburb of Ankara); the generals simply made clear that they would no longer tolerate the Islamist government in power, and Erbakan stepped down.

This bloodless, "postmodern" coup had major, if unintended, consequences. It paved the way for serious soul searching among Turkey's Islamists, eventually causing a generational and ideological rift within their movement. The Welfare Party's pragmatic young leaders, such as Erdogan and Gul, recognized the limits as to how much they could challenge Turkey's secular establishment. Erdogan, then the mayor of Istanbul, had learned the lesson the hard way, having spent four months in jail in 1999 for reciting a poem with militant Islamic undertones. And the secularist backlash against the Welfare Party further convinced moderate Islamist politicians of the benefits of liberal democracy. After having participated in democratic politics for over three decades, they had already learned to temper their views in order to gain electoral legitimacy; by the late 1990s, political Islam was well integrated into the mainstream political system. When, in 2001, Erdogan created the AKP from the ashes of the recently banned Virtue Party (successor to the Welfare Party), it was as a moderate conservative party.

Meanwhile, capitalism and private-sector-driven economic development helped a new religiously conservative base to emerge. The gradual political, social, and economic opening of Turkey under Ozal during the 1980s had created an entrepreneurial Muslim bourgeoisie in the heartland of Anatolia. These middle-class Muslims were globally integrated in terms of their commercial activities but socially and culturally more insular than the elites in Istanbul and Ankara. In time, these small and medium-size business groups—the "Anatolian tigers," as political economists called them—created their own financial networks and challenged the supremacy of the large industrial conglomerates based in Istanbul. By the turn of the millennium, the support of these businesspeople ended up proving crucial in helping the AKP shed its Islamist past and rebrand itself as a pro-market and pro-Western conservative democratic party.

At roughly the same time, EU leaders finally certified Turkey's full eligibility for EU membership, giving the AKP yet another boost. Turkey's candidacy was on track, and Erdogan, who understood that political liberalization would consolidate the AKP's power base, wisely placed the EU's guidelines for democratization at the top of the AKP's agenda. In so doing he achieved two crucial objectives. First, he earned the support of Turkey's business community, liberal intellectuals, and pragmatic middle class. Second, and perhaps more important, he won a semblance of political legitimacy in the eyes of the secularist military; Europe, after all, had been the ultimate prize in Ataturk's vision of a truly Westernized Turkey. By distancing itself from political Islam and embracing democratic and liberal positions, as well as condemning corruption, the AKP also appealed to Turkey's impoverished underclass. The strategy paid off when the party won the 2002 parliamentary elections.

The AKP government soon passed an impressive series of reforms to harmonize Turkey's judicial system, civil-military relations, and human rights practices with European norms. Thanks to its formidable grass-roots network, the AKP was able to provide much-needed social and economic services: it made health care and housing credits more accessible, distributed food, increased grants for students, improved the infrastructure of poorer urban districts, and made the promotion of minority rights for Kurds and non-Muslims alike a priority. Its efforts were not confined to democratization. Following guidelines from the IMF's stabilization program and the economic reform program launched by former finance minister Kemal Dervis, the party also managed to get the Turkish economy back on track after the economic crisis of 2001. Between 2002 and 2007, the Turkish economy grew by an annual average of 7.5 percent. Lower inflation and lower interest rates led to a major increase in domestic consumption, and thanks to a disciplined privatization program, the Turkish economy began to attract unprecedented amounts of foreign direct investment. The average per capita income quadrupled, from just over $2,000 in 2001 to more than $8,000 in 2007, exceeding per capita incomes of some new EU members.[5]

Yet even as the AKP moved close to a more liberal order, the Kemalist segments of Turkish society grew increasingly suspicious that it had a hidden agenda. They feared that the AKP was exploiting the EU membership process to diminish the military's political role and eventually do away with Turkey's Kemalist legacy. They balked, for instance, at AKP measures to increase the ratio of civilians to military officers on the National Security Council, elect a civilian to head the NSC's secretariat, remove military representatives on the boards of the Council of Higher Education and the Radio and Television High Council, and grant Kurds broadcasting and cultural rights.

Another major bone of contention was Prime Minister Erdogan's willingness to compromise on the question of Cyprus. The AKP strongly supported a UN plan to reunify the island; the military adamantly opposed it. Since the deadlock over Cyprus was an important obstacle to Turkey's EU membership prospects, the issue polarized Turkish politics, creating pro-EU and anti-EU camps. The independent magazine *Nokta* revealed in spring 2007 that a military coup over the issue of Cyprus had barely been averted in 2004, due to divisions among the Turkish General Staff's top brass. In retrospect, the AKP seems to have been extremely lucky that the chief of the Turkish General Staff between 2002 and 2006 was Hilmi Ozkok, a general deeply committed to civilian authority over the military; he is said to have restrained hard-liners in his camp.[6]

Today, given Kemalism's own Western emphasis, even the most ardent secularists within the military know they cannot successfully stage a coup against the AKP on the grounds that it has become too pro-Western; thus, their rallying cry has become the party's alleged agenda to Islamize Turkey. The AKP has never hidden its desire to lift the ban on wearing headscarves in universities and end discriminatory measures against graduates of Islamic high schools (such as special criteria for their university entry examinations). Erdogan, moreover, has at times made efforts to satisfy his more zealous religious supporters, as with his clumsy attempt to criminalize adultery in 2004, his appointment of sometimes poorly qualified religious conservatives to official positions (notably the governor of the Turkish central bank), and his attempts to persuade certain municipalities to discourage the sale of alcohol. On balance, however, the AKP has been careful not to challenge the secular establishment head-on and has sought parliamentary consensus on sensitive social issues before taking action.

Despite the overwhelming AKP victory in the July 22, 2007, elections, Turkey's domestic crisis over secularism is far from settled. The country is still deeply divided, and the Kemalist establishment remains as vigilant as ever. Some hard-liners within the secularist establishment see the AKP electoral triumph, culminating in Abdullah Gul's presidency, as a dagger pointed at the heart of Kemalism. The poorly led CHP's lack of support and dismal performance during the July 22, 2007, elections have exacerbated Turkey's political predicament and reinforced the impression that only the Kemalist military or judiciary can provide checks and balances against Islamization. Yet there is reluctance among military leaders to mount a traditional coup. The military leadership knows that whereas past coups were popular because they put an end to civil strife or government corruption, a direct military intervention now against a highly popular and democratically reelected government would generate much resistance. Instead, they are watching the government carefully, sending signals about their determination to prevent Islamization, and letting the judiciary take actions that might make a traditional military intervention unnecessary.

Turkey's domestic divisions would be dangerous enough even if they were taking place at a time of increased Turkish cooperation with its long-standing Western allies. Instead, Turkey has in recent years been getting increasingly frustrated with the very Western countries, the United States and the members of the EU, that it was supposedly trying to join. The United States and

Europe have become less popular with practically all Turks because of their positions on issues such as Iraq, Cyprus, Armenia, and EU membership, and Turkey's military establishment is angry at what it sees as Western sympathy for Kurdish and Islamist movements that they believe threaten the Turkish state. Even as its elites were squabbling over Turkey's domestic order, a major crisis with the United States over Iraq combined with the mounting impression that the EU was closing its door to Turkey have raised real questions about the future of Turkey's Western course.

CHAPTER THREE

The Crisis with the United States

IN A WIDELY publicized poll taken in Turkey in 2002, Turks were asked which country in the world was Turkey's "best friend" in the international arena. The United States placed a respectable second: 27 percent of Turks called America their best friend. Less encouraging was the news that first place went to "nobody," at 33 percent.[1] The poll results said a lot about the Turkish tendency—dating all the way back to the country's isolation in the dying years of the Ottoman Empire—to feel aggrieved in a world in which nobody takes Turkish interests into account. But it also said a lot about the relationship with the United States. Turks clearly felt that if anybody understood them, it was America.

Today that feeling is gone. Indeed, when the same question was asked in a *Turkish Daily News* online poll in 2006, "nobody" was again seen to be Turkey's best friend, this time at 24 percent. But now the European Union was in second place, at 19.3 percent, and the United States had fallen to just 13.2 percent. America was now just a couple of percentage points ahead of the Islamic world and Pakistan on the list of Turkey's best friends.[2]

Other recent polling data on Turkish attitudes toward the United States paint an even more negative picture. Whereas only a few years ago it may have been accurate to say that the United States and Turkey had a trusting strategic partnership, today confidence between the two countries—or at least their populations—has significantly broken down. As recently as the year 2000, 52 percent of Turks said they had a "favorable opinion" of the United States. By 2008, however, that number had fallen to just 12 percent, the lowest level for any of the twenty-four countries surveyed.[3] Other polling data show that 91 percent of Turks disagree with the U.S.-led "global war on terrorism"; only 8 percent of Turks have confidence in President Bush; 82 percent of Turks consider U.S. policies in the Middle East a threat to peace and security; and 81 percent of Turks say it would be "better if another rivaled U.S. military power" compared with just 10 percent who say the opposite.[4] Popular culture also reflected the Turkish mood—the most popular movies and books of 2006 included Burak Turna and Orkun Ucar's novel *Metal Storm*, based on the premise of a U.S. invasion of Turkey, and the film *Valley of the Wolves*, which depicted American soldiers as brutal criminals with little regard for Muslim lives. In mid-2007, no less than 64 percent of Turks named the United States as the country that posed the greatest threat to them, a far higher percentage than in any of the other seven Middle Eastern countries polled.[5]

The United States' unpopularity in Turkey is particularly disturbing in the context of the close and mutually beneficial strategic partnership the two countries have maintained for sixty years. That partnership was born of the common strategic interests generated by the cold war, and specifically the anti-communist priority of both countries. After World War II, the Kemalist establishment needed American support against its communist adversaries within Turkey, and the United States needed Turkey as a Western bulwark against the Soviet Union. The 1947 Truman Doctrine provided for large amounts of U.S. financial assistance to Turkey to fight communists, a favor Turkey returned a few years later when it sent some 25,000 troops to fight alongside U.S. forces under UN auspices in the Korean War. The Turkish troops fought admirably, winning lasting U.S. gratitude and helping to forge the country's image as a solid Western ally. Turkey joined NATO in 1952 and began receiving larger amounts of American economic and military assistance. In 1959 it allowed the United States to station fifteen nuclear-armed Jupiter missiles on its territory as part of the containment of the Soviet Union. When the Turkish military overthrew the elected Menderes government in 1960, the United States looked the other way—the strategic relationship with an anti-Soviet ally was more important than democracy, especially given Menderes's flirtation with Moscow just prior to his ouster.

Convergent strategic interests did not, of course, mean that there were no serious disagreements in the U.S.-Turkey relationship. When Turkish and Greek Cypriots clashed on Cyprus in 1963, President Lyndon Johnson warned Ankara that if military intervention by Turkey (to protect the minority Turkish Cypriot population) provoked a Soviet response, the United States would not feel obliged to uphold its NATO commitment to come to Turkey's defense. The "Johnson Letter" became a lasting source of resentment in Turkey. Following Turkey's military intervention in Cyprus in 1974—which resulted in the division of the island between the Turkish Cypriot north and the Greek Cypriot south—the U.S. Congress froze economic aid and imposed an arms embargo on Turkey that lasted until 1978. Unlike some of its neighbors, moreover, Turkey has never benefited from the presence in the United States of a strong ethnic lobby. Whereas Armenian Americans, Greek Americans, and Greek Cypriot Americans are all very well organized and funded, Turkish Americans have traditionally been neither. To the extent that Turkey has a lobby in the United States at all it has largely been the executive branch of the U.S. government, more attuned to geopolitics than Congress.

Given the origins of the U.S.-Turkey strategic relationship, it was reasonable to fear that the end of the cold war—the disappearance of the Soviet Union as a common threat—would threaten its future. In fact, the opposite happened. It is true that the 1990–91 Gulf war strained the U.S.-Turkey partnership and led to significant Turkish complaints that Turkey was not adequately compensated for the costs of the war. (According to Turks this included supporting 450,000 Kurdish refugees in Turkey and over $35 billion in lost economic revenues to sanctions, experiences that would be foremost in Turkish minds ten years later, when the United States made new promises to compensate Turkey for the costs of a war in Iraq.) But even as it led to tensions, the Gulf war also strengthened the U.S.-Turkey partnership by making Turkey even more strategically valuable to the United States. As Washington turned toward a regime of containment of Saddam Hussein, Turkish cooperation with sanctions and its provision of military bases became essential.

Indeed, far from crumbling, the U.S.-Turkey strategic partnership blossomed in the 1990s. Driven both by the need for Turkish cooperation in Iraq and by the desire to help stabilize a large and strategically placed democracy, the Clinton administration stood by Turkey on a number of critical issues. It backed Turkish loan guarantees from the International Monetary Fund, designated Turkey as a "Big Emerging Market," pushed for new pipelines to be built across Turkey to get Caspian oil and gas to the Mediterranean, strongly supported Turkey's membership in the European Union, and authorized ongoing arms sales to Turkey, often in the face of pressure from domestic lobbies against doing so.

In many ways the high point of the U.S.-Turkey partnership came in 1999. In February of that year, U.S. intelligence officials helped Turkey capture the PKK leader Abdullah Ocalan after a Turkish threat of military intervention had driven him from his sanctuary in Syria. The United States' role in Ocalan's capture was widely reported in Turkey and earned the Americans great appreciation. In November 1999, President Clinton spent five days in Turkey on a bilateral visit to Ankara and to attend an Organization for Security and Cooperation in Europe (OSCE) summit held in Istanbul. Whereas Clinton's abbreviated visit to Greece on the way to Turkey was marred by widespread street protests (the Greeks were angry about the war in Kosovo), Clinton was widely applauded in Turkey, especially after he made a historic speech to the Turkish parliament and visited survivors of a tragic earthquake. The contrast between the youthful Clinton mingling with crowds and Turkey's own leadership–the seventy-four-year-old Bulent Ecevit had been widely criticized for his slow and inefficient response to the earthquake–was striking to the Turks. Finally, in December, Clinton intervened with the Europeans and at the last minute helped secure EU candidacy status for Turkey, yet another sign of a flourishing U.S.-Turkey partnership. All this cooperation based on mutual interest created a sense on both sides that the U.S.-Turkey partnership was so close that neither side would ever risk letting it fall apart. But that is precisely what began to happen in the years to come.

The Split over Iraq

By far the biggest reason for the split between the United States and Turkey was the U.S. invasion of Iraq. After the 9/11 attacks, Turkey stood by the United States and strongly supported the American response in Afghanistan. Indeed, after the fall of the

Taliban, as the U.S. military began looking for supporters of a peacekeeping mission, Turkey took the lead and in early 2002 became the first country to take command of NATO's International Security and Assistance Force (ISAF). As Washington started to train its sites on Iraq later that year, however, Turkey expressed its strong opposition. For Turks, a U.S. invasion of Iraq risked creating an independent Kurdish entity in northern Iraq that could stoke separatist feelings among Turkey's own Kurdish population. With memories of the first Gulf war (with the inflow of refugees and economic costs) still fresh in their minds, the Turkish population strongly opposed another Iraq war.

The U.S.-Turkish differences over the war came to a head in early 2003, when Turkey was pressed to respond to a U.S. request to pre-position the Fourth Armored Division in Turkey for a potential invasion of Iraq from the north. The AKP government that had been elected in November 2002 wanted to establish its pro-Western credentials and help the United States. But it also knew that it was viewed with suspicion for its Islamist roots, that it had already provoked Turkish nationalists by trying to promote a compromise on Cyprus, and that many of its core constituents would see the war as unnecessary Western violence against innocent Muslims. The government put off the parliamentary vote on whether to allow U.S. access several times and entered into negotiations with the Americans over how Turkey would be compensated for its cooperation. The negotiations were difficult and often acrimonious—the Americans thought Turkey should have been more ready to contribute to the cause of getting rid of Saddam Hussein and to help its strong American partner, whereas the Turks resented the notion that they could be "bribed" into supporting a war they considered ill advised. The talks eventually resulted in a U.S. offer to provide Turkey with a $6 billion assistance package that could be leveraged to support $24 billion in loan guarantees; in return Turkey agreed to grant the American military access to its territory for staging purposes; the U.S. agreed that some 20,000 Turkish troops could enter northern Iraq to protect Turkish interests there.[6]

But on March 1, 2003, the Turkish parliament surprised the Americans (and perhaps itself) when it voted to reject the deal. In fact, more deputies (264) voted in favor of the motion to approve U.S. access than against (250), but 19 abstentions meant that the motion did not receive the required majority of votes cast (267 of the 533 votes cast) and failed. For hours after the vote, numerous members of parliament believed that the measure had passed, not realizing that it required a majority of all votes cast rather than of votes for or against.[7] Despite the closeness of the vote, the final result shattered the assumption on both sides that such a serious divergence could never arise between the United States and Turkey. The vote also revealed for the first time the degree to which Turkey's "Islamists" were becoming the pro-Western faction while the traditional secularist establishment was moving in the opposite direction. Whereas a strong majority of AKP deputies followed Prime Minister Erdogan's call to support the deal with the Americans, all of the Kemalist CHP voted against it and the Turkish military failed to speak out in favor of it. Many leading Kemalists with long-standing ties to the United States—including a former Turkish ambassador to the United States (Sukru Elekdag), a former Turkish ambassador to NATO (Onur Oymen), a former vice president of the World Bank (Kemal Dervis), and a former Turkish foreign minister (Ismail Cem)—actively lobbied against it.

The shock and disappointment in the United States were palpable. Tommy Franks, commander of CENTCOM (Central Command), made clear prior to the vote that he would be outraged if Turkey refused to grant the Americans access, and after the vote,

Deputy Secretary of Defense Paul Wolfowitz complained that the Turkish military "did not play the strong leadership role we would have expected."[8] Two years later Defense Secretary Donald Rumsfeld was still attributing the Iraqi insurgency to Turkey's refusal to provide access to American troops, stating: "Had we been successful in getting the 4th Infantry Division to come in through Turkey in the north when our forces were coming up from the south out of Kuwait, I believe that a considerably smaller number of the Ba'athists and the regime elements would have escaped. More would have been captured or killed, and as a result, the insurgency would have been at a lesser intensity than it is today."[9]

Relations between Turkey and the United States over Iraq got even worse on July 4, 2003, when U.S. army forces in northern Iraq detained eleven Turkish special forces commandos suspected of planning to participate in the assassination of a local Kurdish politician. The Turks were released after forty-eight hours, but not before they were photographed hooded and treated as prisoners by the Americans, causing great humiliation and resentment in Turkey. The Turkish General Staff spoke of "the worst crisis of confidence" between Ankara and Washington for more than fifty years, and then Foreign Minister Gul warned that "this harm cannot be forgotten."[10] Although the two sides eventually issued a joint statement of regret about the incident, for many Turks "July 4" came to symbolize America's hostility to Turkey in the same way that for many Americans "March 1" came to symbolize Turkey's lack of support for the United States.

In the months that followed, American military actions in Iraq were increasingly denounced in Turkey. The Turkish press was filled with accusations of American human rights abuses and speculation about alleged U.S. use of chemical or biological weapons in Iraq. After the U.S. Marines assaulted an insurgent stronghold in Fallujah, one prominent AKP member of parliament, Mehmet Elkatmis, insisted that "such a genocide was never seen in the time of the pharaohs, nor of Hitler or of Mussolini."[11] Another Turkish lawmaker, from Adana province (home to the Incirlik airbase), complained, "The U.S. sees [Turkey] not as a strategic partner, but as a logistical partner" and called on Turkey to "suspend our ties with the United States. If we remain silent, we will be tainted by America's tyranny."[12] Erdogan himself referred to the Iraqi insurgents who died in the U.S. assault on Fallujah as "martyrs" and exhorted the Muslim world to unite behind Turkey "against powers that are seeking to assert their hegemony."[13] The strategic partnership that was supposed to bind the two countries together was crumbling under the pressures of the war in Iraq.

Differences over Israel, Armenia, and the Kurds

Other issues added to the growing bilateral tensions. In February 2006, seeking to restore credibility among Islamist voters, Turkey became the first country to receive the Hamas leader Khaled Meshaal following his party's victory in Palestinian elections. The Bush administration avoided direct public criticism of a meeting that undermined its efforts to isolate Hamas and instead called on Turkey to send a "message about abandoning terrorism, recognizing the right of Israel to exist, and adhering to the commitments that the Palestinian Authority has made."[14] But Americans outside of government—including Jewish groups who had supported Turkey as a friend of Israel and who were increasingly worried about reports of anti-Semitism in Turkey—were less restrained. Representatives of the American Jewish Committee called the meeting a "tragic mistake" that would have "serious repercussions not only among the governments of Western democracies but the Jewish community in the United States and around the world and with those friends of Turkey."[15] Former State Department official Henri Barkey underscored how the meeting contrasted with Turkey's approach to other terrorist groups: "By hosting the leader of a terrorist organization—one that has taken terror to new heights with its suicide bombings of malls and city buses—Turkey undermined its own cause. After all, Turkey has for many years been campaigning to get its home-grown Kurdish insurgency classified as a terrorist group. The United States and European Union have done so. So the invitation to the Hamas leader was particularly strange coming from Turkey, even while Turkey is negotiating to join the EU."[16]

Relations with the United States further deteriorated in the summer of 2006 when Turkish leaders denounced America's failure to call for a cease-fire during Israel's war with Hezbollah in Lebanon. Prime Minister Erdogan said that it was "unthinkable to remain silent in the face of this new understanding of power, this new culture of violence which defiles the sense of justice," and that the war was "fuelling violence and further strengthening terrorism."[17] And Foreign Minister Gul warned that U.S. support for Israel's actions could turn Turks and others in the Middle East even further against the United States. "Moderate liberal people [in Turkey] are becoming anti-American and anti-EU," Gul warned. "If our young, dynamic, educated and economically active people become bitter, if their attitudes and feelings are changed, it is not good. Their feeling has changed towards these global policies and strategic issues. This is dangerous."[18]

In this tense climate, the Turkish domestic political crises of 2007 also did little to bring the two countries back together. As the Kemalists and the AKP feuded in the run-up to the presidential election, each side accused the United States of failing to stand up for the principles it held most dear—"secularism" for the

Kemalists and "democracy" for the AKP. For the former, Washington had an undue sympathy for the Erdogan government and—wrongly, in their view—hoped to promote "moderate Islamism" as a "model" that might be adopted in other parts of the Muslim world. The Kemalists argued that the AKP was a wolf in sheep's clothing and that the Americans failed to see the true nature of the Islamist threat. The AKP, for its part, was disappointed that the Bush administration, notwithstanding its "democracy agenda," failed to take a clear stand against a potential military coup against an elected government. Senior AKP members of parliament complained that they had "lost faith in the United States."[19]

By the end of 2007, U.S.-Turkey relations had descended to new depths, as reflected in the public opinion figures previously cited. On October 10, the Foreign Affairs Committee of the House of Representatives voted 27–21 in support of a resolution recognizing an Armenian genocide. As Speaker Nancy Pelosi pledged to bring the measure to the full House for a vote, General Mehmet Yasar Buyukanit warned that Turkey's "military relations with the U.S. would never be as they were in the past" if the House passed the measure and said that the United States had "shot itself in the foot." In an October poll in Turkey, 73 percent of Turks surveyed said that if the House passed the resolution, their opinion of the United States would decline, and 83 percent said that they would oppose Turkish assistance to the United States in Iraq.[20] By the end of October, support for the resolution had faded under heavy pressure from Turkey and the Bush administration, but significant damage had been done and the issue would continue to loom over the relationship.

Finally, nothing did more to strain U.S.-Turkish ties than the growing resentment in Turkey over the Kurdish issue. With PKK violence rising again after having fallen for several years, resentful

Turks increasingly blamed the United States for having provoked Kurdish separatism with its invasion of Iraq and for failing to do more to stop it. In October 2007, Turkey began massing forces on the Iraqi border, regularly shelling suspected PKK sites, and insisting that if Washington or Iraqi Kurdish leaders did not crack down on the PKK the Turkish army would do so itself. On October 17, the Turkish parliament voted overwhelmingly to authorize a military incursion into Iraq, while the United States, fearing that such an incursion could destabilize the one part of Iraq that was relatively peaceful, strongly opposed it. President Bush noted—with no obvious irony—"We are making it very clear to Turkey that we don't think it is in their interests to send troops into Iraq."[21]

By November, the U.S. refusal to support Turkish military action in northern Iraq was becoming almost untenable in terms of its effect on U.S.-Turkey relations and led to a stronger U.S. line on the PKK. Speaking in Ankara on November 2, Secretary of State Condoleezza Rice stated that PKK terrorism was a "common threat" to the United States and Turkey, and a few days later President Bush told Prime Minister Erdogan that the United States would share more intelligence with Turkey.[22] By December, after a series of particularly violent PKK attacks that killed more than forty Turkish civilians and soldiers, Washington had abandoned its opposition to Turkish cross-border operations and backed Turkey, both politically and with actionable intelligence, as it undertook air strikes and raids on PKK positions in northern Iraq.

The U.S. support for Turkish military action was appreciated in Ankara, with newly elected President Gul commenting that "we should have come to this point earlier."[23] But the boost to U.S.-Turkey relations was short-lived, and the greater American willingness to help Turkey could not overcome the grave suspicions among many Turks that Washington was in fact sympathetic to Kurdish nationalist aspirations and would ultimately support an independent Kurdish state. Those suspicions were deepened by American pressure on Turkey, after a new offensive in February 2008, to limit the duration of its operations in Iraq to "a week or two," in the words of Secretary of Defense Robert Gates, and calls by senior U.S. military officials, including Lieutenant General Ray Odierno, the former commander of the Multi-National Corps in Iraq, for Turkey to "talk and have negotiations with these terrorist elements [the PKK]."[24] On March 5, shortly after Turkey's military incursion came to an end, Admiral William Fallon, then commander of the U.S. Central Command, stated at a hearing of the House Armed Services Committee that he believed the solution to the PKK issue lay in reaching "some kind of accommodation" with the organization.[25]

For nearly fifty years, despite sometimes serious differences, the United States and Turkey each always assumed it could count on the other in the name of common strategic interests. The U.S.-Turkish split over Iraq—coming on top of major differences over Israel, Armenia, Cyprus, and other issues—suggested that the era in which that assumption held had come to an end.

CHAPTER FOUR

Europe's Closing Door

THE CRISIS IN U.S.-Turkey relations would perhaps be less dramatic if Turkey's relationship with Europe were stable or improving. Instead, however, Turkey's prospects for joining the European Union—a long-standing dream—seem to be fading at the very time that its relationship with Washington is also coming under strain. The coincidence of these two factors hardly bodes well for the future of Turkey's Western orientation.

Turkey's quest to become part of Europe predates the EU, and even the establishment of modern Turkey. This may seem surprising, because the Ottoman Empire was the traditional enemy of Europe, the external threat that played a crucial role in consolidating Europe's Christian identity. Yet as centuries of Ottoman splendor came to an end, the ruling elite of Istanbul sought salvation in Westernization. Ottoman reforms in the military, legal, and political fields were pragmatically modeled on Europe. But Ottoman modernization proved too little too late to save the empire. Torn between Islamic pride and the imperative of Westernization, Ottomans developed a split identity in the nineteenth century, during which modern and traditional institutions ineffectively coexisted.

A more radical version of Westernization came only during the first half of the twentieth century, first under the Young Turks and later with Ataturk. As the founder of the fledgling Turkish Republic, Ataturk was firmly convinced that his country needed to become part of "contemporary civilization." Having set the course toward the West, Turkey subsequently became an integral member of the Western alliance and a frontline state against the Soviet Union. The economy of the new Turkey, at the edge of Europe, naturally gravitated toward Europe as well. The impulse to belong to Europe gained further momentum with the collapse of the Soviet Union. Ankara increasingly felt that its place in the New World Order was in the progressive and increasingly democratic institutions that Europe represented. For many Turks, joining the European Union became synonymous with the final push toward realizing Ataturk's dream of joining contemporary civilization. For them, Turkey as a member of the EU would become economically prosperous as well as politically stable and democratic.

Turkey's path toward Europe was full of obstacles, and Europeans never shared Americans' unqualified enthusiasm for the prospect of Turkey as a full member of the EU. Throughout the cold war, while the United States saw Turkey's potential EU membership in geopolitical terms, Europeans worried about Turkey's potential cultural, social, and economic impact on their own societies. In the eyes of most Europeans Turkey is simply too big (with a larger population than every EU member state except Germany), too poor (a per capita GDP less than one-third of the EU average), and too different (99 percent Muslim) to qualify as a member. Political instability within Turkey itself was another obstacle. Although Turkey applied for European membership in

1963, the military interventions against democratically elected governments in 1971 and 1980 seriously undermined Ankara's chances.

But Turkey had one major factor going in its favor during these difficult decades: the cold war. As a NATO member country that shared borders with the Soviet Union and tied down some twenty-four Russian divisions, Turkey's credentials as a valuable military asset to the West were undisputed. Thorny questions about democratic standards, military interventions, human rights, and Muslim identity were set aside.

This somewhat uncomplicated Western image of Turkey lasted as long as the cold war did. But to Ankara's dismay, after the demise of the Soviet Union Turkish democracy came under increasingly critical scrutiny. Moreover, by the early 1990s, Central and Eastern Europe had emerged as more pressing priorities for EU enlargement. At a time when Europe seemed to regret its cold war commitments to Turkey, Ankara urgently wanted to be anchored in the West, not least because of potentially destabilizing factors within Turkey, the Balkans, the Caucasus, and the Middle East. Now that communism and the Soviets had vanished, deeply rooted ethnic and religious rivalries were no longer masked by left-right ideological cleavages.

As a result, just as Europe was turning its back on Turkey, Ankara increasingly came to see its EU membership as the guarantor and litmus test of Western identity, national prestige, and economic prosperity. Yet instead of displaying the democratic and liberal credentials necessary for such membership, Turkey became politically polarized under the pressure of its own internal contradictions. The war against the PKK and the ousting of the Islamist prime minister Necmettin Erbakan caused domestic unrest and undermined Turkey's image. Political instability plagued the Turkish economy, which suffered from corruption, clientelism, and hyperinflation. For the most part, relations with the European Union reflected this negative turn of events. The only significant progress during this period came in the form of a Customs Union with the EU, strongly backed by the United States—and many Turks—as a step toward Turkey's eventual EU membership. At the Luxembourg Summit in December 1997, however, the EU decided to exclude Turkey from its enlargement process, refusing even to recognize it as an official "candidate" for EU membership. Instead, it was placed in a special category, behind twelve other aspiring members from Central and Eastern Europe.

The snub at Luxembourg led an increasingly frustrated Ankara to take the unprecedented step of suspending its political relations with the EU. Turkey's frustration to a large extent focused on European Christian Democrats, and especially the Helmut Kohl government in Germany. Only a few months before the Luxembourg Summit, in March 1997, the European Christian Democratic Union (CDU), the body representing all Christian Democratic political parties in Western Europe, had declared that "the EU is in the process of building a civilization in which Turkey has no place."[1] In December 1997, the Luxembourg Summit's *Agenda 2000* declared that the EU would put Turkey in a special category of its own, in the framework of a new "European strategy" for Ankara. This stance vis-à-vis Turkey reflected categorical opposition to Turkey's full EU membership: a view shared by Kohl's CDU, one of the signatories of the European Christian Democratic declaration. Then Turkish Prime Minister Mesut Yilmaz, educated in Germany and fluent in German, singled out the Kohl government in his accusations, going so far as to accuse the Kohl government of following a policy of "Lebensraum," because of its support for EU enlargement to Eastern Europe but not to Muslim Turkey.[2] (These bitter feelings would foreshadow the way many

Turks would feel years later, when the German CDU's new leadership, under Chancellor Angela Merkel, adopted a position similarly hostile to Turkey's EU hopes.)

The crisis lasted for two years, until the EU finally changed course by officially approving Turkey's "candidacy" status at the Helsinki Summit in December 1999.[3] The change in the EU's position was made possible largely thanks to a series of new developments in Turkey, coupled with more favorable dynamics in Europe. On the domestic side, by early 1999, PKK leader Abdullah Ocalan was behind bars and his separatist movement, largely defeated. Fifteen years of intense guerrilla warfare came to an end with a great sense of national victory. Also by 1999, the military had already forced the Islamic Welfare Party out of power with the "soft coup" against Prime Minister Erbakan. With Kurdish separatism at least temporarily defeated and political Islam subdued, the sense of siege that characterized the 1990s had finally come to an end, helping to create positive momentum for reforms from a position of strength rather than weakness.

External factors also contributed to the progress with Europe. In 1998 a change of government in Germany ended sixteen years of Christian Democratic rule and ushered in an SPD-Green coalition much more open to potential EU membership for Turkey. Turkey's relations with Greece were also improving rapidly, as a new government in Athens acted on the premise that a resentful and excluded neighbor was not in its national interest. Earthquakes in Istanbul and Athens in August and September 1999 also triggered significant goodwill and sympathy between the two countries—each of which rushed to send emergency rescue workers to the other in its hours of need. Over the following few years Greece evolved from being an ardent foe of Turkey's EU membership to being a strong supporter of it. Finally, the United States lobbied Europeans heavily in favor of Turkey during 1998 and 1999, including phone calls from President Clinton to European leaders during the Helsinki Summit. All these factors significantly improved the atmospherics in Turkey and Europe, and the EU confirmed Ankara's candidacy for membership.

Stimulated in part by this more realistic desire to qualify for membership, Ankara began implementing a series of economic and political reforms, especially after the new finance minister, Kemal Dervis, backed by the International Monetary Fund, helped Turkey recover from a severe financial crisis in 2001. The impact of improved relations between Turkey and the EU became most evident during the 2002 elections. For the first time in Turkish history, a political party with Islamic roots—the AKP—won a majority of seats in national parliamentary elections. More important, the AKP won by adopting an aggressively pro-EU political platform. By declaring Turkey's EU membership as its top priority, Turkey's reformed Islamic movement managed to achieve two crucial objectives: it gained a sense of political legitimacy in the eyes of Turkey's secular traditionalists while winning the support of Turkey's pragmatic middle class, business community, and liberal intellectuals.

The AKP enjoyed great popularity with working-class Turks, but without its strong commitment to EU membership and the Kemalist state's desire to be part of Europe, the party would still have lacked political legitimacy. In that sense, the AKP owed its electoral victory in large part to Turkey's European vocation. After its victory in November 2002, the AKP leadership committed itself to a democratic reform process guided by the EU's "Copenhagen Criteria" for membership, which include democratic institutions, commitment to human rights, a functioning market economy, and an ability to meet EU membership obligations. To meet these criteria, the government built on efforts begun under the previous government and passed an impressive series of liberal reforms, including bolstering civilian control of the powerful National Security Council (and publishing the council's deliberations); improving human rights and freedom of speech; working to prevent torture and prisoner abuse; allowing limited broadcasting and language instruction rights for Kurds and other minorities; abolishing the State Security Courts, which had been set up after the military coup in 1980; allowing for the retrial of legal cases where verdicts were rejected by the European Court of Human Rights; and further liberalizing the economy. In December 2002, the European Council, on the basis of a report and recommendation from the European Commission, decided that Turkey fulfilled the Copenhagen Criteria and agreed to open accession negotiations with Turkey "without delay." These developments all contributed to growing optimism in Turkey that progress toward EU membership was being made.

New Setbacks

Over the past few years, however, that progress has stalled and the optimism faded, for several reasons. One was the growing sense of "enlargement fatigue" in Europe, especially following the May 2004 accession of ten new EU members. Many European citizens were opposed to such an influx of new members, about which they were not consulted, a fact that hardly left them enthusiastic about taking in Turkey, whose population alone was almost as large as that of all these new members put together. The fact that one of the new, veto-wielding EU members was the Greek Cypriot–led Republic of Cyprus hardly augured well for Turkey's own accession aspirations.

Making matters worse, in the summer of 2005 the EU entered a period of political crisis following the French and Dutch rejections of the proposed EU constitution, in no small part because of public insecurities about unemployment and immigration. Furthermore, in a quixotic and ultimately futile effort to reassure public opinion before the vote on the EU constitution, France changed its constitution to require that any further EU enlargement require a referendum, a potentially huge future obstacle to Turkey. The summer of 2005 also saw horrific terrorist attacks in Britain by Muslim extremists, following those in Madrid the previous year (as well as the murder by an Islamist of the Dutch filmmaker Theo van Gogh), which only increased European concerns about radical Islam and terrorism and further diminished enthusiasm for open borders with Turkey. By this time, only 30 percent of EU citizens were in favor of Turkish membership, and 52 percent were against. Large majorities in opposition to Turkish membership in Cyprus (80 percent), Austria (80 percent), Germany (74 percent), and France (68 percent) raised real questions about whether those countries' leaders would ever support Turkey's eventual accession.[4]

In October 2005, after brutal internal debate, the EU did agree to start accession negotiations with Turkey, in theory a hugely positive step, as no aspiring EU member had ever started the accession negotiating process without eventually concluding it. Whatever celebrations the Turks may have held following that EU decision, however, were short-lived, and the difficulties in getting the positive EU decision on accession talks should have been seen as a warning that the path to actual membership would hardly be smooth. After ultimately resisting Cyprus's efforts to require Turkey, as part of the accession process, to recognize its Greek Cypriot–led government and overcoming Austria's determination to offer Turkey a "privileged partnership" instead of membership, the EU added some important caveats to its decision to start talks. It noted that the talks could be "open-ended," that Turkey's eventual membership would depend on the EU's "absorption capacity," and that "permanent safeguards" could be required on issues ranging from freedom of movement to regional aid.[5] While none of these qualifications was new, most Turks read them as clear signals that although the EU would grudgingly agree to start accession talks, it would not necessarily agree to end them by granting accession.

On top of all this was the Cyprus issue itself, which was already contributing to Turkey's sense of alienation from the EU. In 2003 the AKP government took enormous domestic political risks and reversed long-standing Turkish policy by pressing the Turkish Cypriots to accept a political compromise on the island, which would, the government hoped, enhance Turkey's chances of joining the EU. The Turkish Cypriots supported the UN-sponsored "Annan Plan" in an April 2004 referendum, which the Greek Cypriot side rejected.[6] Yet despite American and European claims that there would be negative consequences for any side that rejected the plan and rewards for those who supported it, neither the EU nor the United States has entirely fulfilled its pledges to "put an end to the isolation of the Turkish Cypriot community," as the EU foreign ministers put it.[7] After the Greek Cypriots rejected the Annan Plan, EU member states agreed to open direct, duty-free trade with Turkish Cypriots and to set aside some €259 million for infrastructure and private-sector development in the Turkish Cypriot north, but the Greek Cypriots blocked the agreement. Nearly two years later, the EU used a qualified majority voting procedure (not possible regarding the direct-trade issue) to disburse the funding, but has not been able to spend most of it, again because of limits the officially recognized Greek Cypriot government has imposed. The Turkish Cypriots thus still suffer from international isolation while the Greek Cypriots now use Cyprus's membership in the EU to demand concessions from Turkey and to continue to isolate northern Cyprus. Meanwhile, the AKP government has to fend off charges back home that it sold out its Turkish brethren while getting little in return.[8]

Such a perception is compounded by the fact that the Erdogan government agreed on July 29, 2005, to extend its Customs Union with the EU to the newest EU members, including Cyprus, as a precondition to start accession negotiations with Brussels. Prime Minister Erdogan made clear, however, that he is not prepared to open Turkey's ports to Greek-Cypriot-flagged vessels, as required by the EU, unless the EU fulfills its promise to ease the isolation of the Turkish Cypriots. As a result, in December 2006 Cyprus tried to stop negotiations with Turkey and got the EU to agree to partial suspension of accession negotiations between Ankara and Brussels. To accede to the EU, an aspiring member must complete detailed negotiations in thirty-five different issue areas called "chapters," which include taxation, financial services, energy, transport, and foreign, security, and defense policy. As of spring 2008, eight of the chapters related to foreign policy and trade issues have remained frozen. The situation is likely to remain blocked as long as no progress is made on the Cyprus dispute. Greek Cypriots like to point out that they will have at least seventy opportunities over the next ten years to block Turkish accession, one for each time the EU opens and closes one of the chapters of negotiations.

A further consequence of the Cyprus stalemate is that it prevents NATO and the EU from expanding their institutional cooperation, to the detriment not only of international security but also of Turkey's EU prospects. Because of the Cyprus dispute, Cyprus, a member of the EU, refuses to allow Turkey to take part in discussions of EU security missions, and Turkey, a member of NATO, does the same on the NATO side. The absurd result is that when the two organizations meet they briefly discuss the one common operation they have agreed on, in Bosnia and Herzegovina, before immediately adjourning the meeting. This situation hardly contributes to a strengthening of the ties between Turkey and the EU.

Finally, Turkey's EU prospects were seriously set back by the November 2005 election of Chancellor Angela Merkel in Germany and the May 2007 election of President Nicolas Sarkozy in France. Merkel broke with the previous SPD government's support for eventual Turkish membership and advocates the alternative of a "privileged partnership," while Sarkozy campaigned on a position of strong opposition to Turkish membership in the EU. Appealing to the majority of French who oppose Turkish accession, Sarkozy argues that Turkey is "not a European country" and insists that EU membership for Turkey would "kill the very idea of European integration."[9] In 2008 Sarkozy promoted a constitutional change in France that would lift the requirement of a referendum for EU enlargement to other countries but maintain that requirement for Turkey.[10] So long as these two leaders are in power in two of the EU's most important countries—barring a major change of heart—Turkey has little chance of joining the EU.

The result of all these developments is that Turks now no longer believe they will get into the EU—and fewer than ever even want to. Opinion polls show that only 43 percent of Turks now see EU membership as a "good thing," and only 26 percent actually believe Turkey will ever become a full member, almost 50 percent lower than only five years ago.[11] According to a 2007 Eurobarometer survey, only 25 percent of Turks now trust the EU, down sixteen points from the previous year.[12] Given its already troubled partnership with the United States, Turkey's growing frustration with Europe is alarming. For the first time in its history, the Turkish Republic has serious problems with the United States and the European Union at the same time.

CHAPTER FIVE

Turkey's Eurasian Alternatives

THE PROSPECT OF Turkey's turning away from the West should not be exaggerated. Turks on both sides of the secular-religious divide still value their relations with the United States and Europe and understand the costs of isolation and the limits of their geopolitical alternatives. But Turkey's close relations with the West should not be taken for granted either. As we have seen, deep resentment of America's Iraq policy and fading hopes of EU membership have increased Turkish frustration with the West and provoked a nationalist reaction across the Turkish political spectrum. Many conservative AKP supporters resent America's Middle East policy and Europe's unwillingness to embrace Turkey. At the same time, Turkey's Kemalist establishment is suspicious of Westerners they believe are naively soft on Islamists and dangerously tolerant of Kurdish nationalism.

A growing sense of self-confidence and self-importance is also contributing to Turkey's mounting nationalism and frustration with the West. After five years of political stability and high economic growth between 2002 and 2007, most Turks are optimistic about their country's status as a power in the region and the world. Turkey has become the fifth largest economy in Europe and one of the twenty largest economies in the world. Income per capita has recently reached the critical threshold of $10,000—a threefold increase since 2000. Thanks to better governance and a growing acceptance of capitalism in Anatolia, the country's social, economic, and cultural life is vibrant. The Turkish private sector is extremely entrepreneurial and productive. Turkey's combined geostrategic significance and military power—Turkey has the second largest army in NATO—fuel a sense among Turks that they should not be junior partners in an alliance with the West. In other words, an increasingly self-confident Turkey demands respect, and many Turks feel they have not been getting respect from Europe and the United States.

One consequence of these trends has been a conscious Turkish effort in recent years to play a greater role in Middle East diplomacy and to strengthen its ties to other regional actors, from Russia to Syria to Iran—sometimes to the distinct displeasure of the United States. Turkish officials do not claim to see their future more closely aligned with these states than with their Western partners, but they are sending a clear message to the West that Turkey will pursue its own perceived interests, not those determined by Washington. Prime Minister Erdogan has demonstrated this repeatedly in recent years by taking positions at odds with the United States on issues such as Israel's targeted killings of Palestinian militants, the Israel-Lebanon war in the summer of 2006, and the diplomatic isolation of Hamas.[1]

Since the AKP came to power in November 2002, its foreign policy has been based on what Erdogan's top foreign policy adviser, Ahmet Davutoglu, calls "strategic depth."[2] Davutoglu, formerly a professor of international relations at universities in Turkey and Malaysia, argues that in the past, Turkish foreign policy was unbalanced, with an overemphasis on ties with Western

Europe and the United States to the neglect of Turkey's interests with other countries, particularly in the Middle East. Now it is a "central country with multiple regional identities that cannot be reduced to one, unified category." [3] He argues that the Turkish Republic, the successor state of the Ottoman Empire, unlike other former imperial powers, for the first eighty years after its foundation in 1923 largely ignored relations with the independent states that had been formed out of the former Ottoman provinces in North Africa and the Middle East, and that Turkey today needs to play a greater role in these countries.

Davutoglu's "neo-Ottoman" vision, it should be noted, is very different from that promulgated in the late 1990s by Islamist prime minister Necmettin Erbakan. Whereas Erbakan sought to create an Islamic alliance with Muslim countries such as Libya, Iran, Malaysia, and Indonesia as an explicit alternative to the West, AKP leaders today want to reach out to the East to complement their ties to the West, not replace them. Their vision, which builds on the approach of former President Turgut Ozal (and was already then labeled "neo-Ottomanism"), is one in which Turkey rediscovers its imperial legacy and seeks a new national consensus within which the country's multiple identities can coexist. It reminds Turks that they once had a great multinational empire that ruled the Middle East, North Africa, the Balkans, and parts of Central Europe. In other words, this new emphasis on the Ottoman legacy is not about Islamization but rather about counterbalancing what its proponents see as Kemalism's obsession with Turkey's Western identity.

Much of Turkey's secular elite fears that the notion of neo-Ottomanism is merely cover for an Islamist agenda that would sideline the military's traditional role of the guardian of secularism. But the secularists, now themselves disgruntled with the West, have their own reasons for reaching out to other states in the region with which they share common strategic interests, sometimes even more than with their traditional partners in the West. As one prominent retired general argued in a May 2007 speech, the new strategic situation means that "Turkey should leave the NATO alliance and search possibilities for close co-operation with Russia and other power centers in the region."[4] If proponents of this view were to take power in Turkey, especially in the context of a judicial or a military coup that led to political sanctions from Europe or the United States, they might well seek to further develop their relations with authoritarian states in the region and beyond. For the most militant secularists, that outcome might even be preferred to retaining close ties to a West they no longer trust.

As Turkey considers potential partners outside the Western world, where might it look? A consideration of Turkish diplomacy over the past several years suggests several options.

Russia

Turkish-Russian relations are undergoing a significant rapprochement for a number of reasons. For most of the 1990s, Moscow viewed Turkey as a proxy for the United States. Turkey encroached on Russia's position in the Caucasus and Central Asia by playing on its historic associations with the Turkic Muslim peoples of the regions. Russia and Turkey were in opposing camps on issues such as Bosnia, Kosovo, and Chechnya, in large part because of the Balkan and Caucasian diasporas in Turkey. And Russia saw American efforts to transform Turkey into a transit corridor for Caspian energy exports (especially oil and gas from Azerbaijan) to Europe as a strategic threat to its interests.

This tense bilateral relationship began to improve considerably in 2003. After the U.S. invasion of Iraq, Turkey's and Russia's common frustration with Washington began to translate into a shared vision of regional problems and common concerns about American power and policy. President Putin and Prime Minister Erdogan began to coordinate their policies toward Iran, Syria, and other states in the Middle East where Russia hopes to regain some of the position it lost with the collapse of the Soviet Union. In Iran, for example, Turkey's interests appear to be more in line with Russia's interests than with those of the United States. Although Turkish officials profess concern about Iran's nuclear program, Turkey is, like Russia, reluctant to support significant diplomatic or economic sanctions on Tehran. The hard-line U.S. approach to Iran troubles most Turks, who fear American military action against another neighbor will further destabilize the region. In 2007 the Turkish government reiterated its determination to press ahead with major investments in the Iranian energy sector, despite U.S. opposition.

Closer to home, Russia and Turkey have resisted U.S. involvement in the Istanbul-based Black Sea Economic Cooperation organization (BSEC), and Russia is trying to exploit its new relationship with Turkey to complicate American support for Georgia's membership in NATO. Perhaps most important, once-divisive issues such as Chechnya and the Kurds have gradually faded in importance. In early 2005, Putin and Erdogan, expressing similar fears of terrorism and separatism, reportedly reached an agreement to support each other's positions on Chechnya and the Kurds.[5] This is a far cry from the 1990s, when the Turkish government turned a blind eye to its Chechen population's active support for the Chechen cause and Russia allowed Kurdish associations with links to the PKK to operate in Moscow.

Finally, Turkey's economic relationship with Russia is improving significantly. The trade volume between the two countries is now at an all-time high, having risen from $10 billion in 2004 to

$20 billion in 2007. Russia now accounts for more than 70 percent of Turkish gas imports (the major item in bilateral trade), thanks to a dedicated gas export pipeline, Blue Stream, between the two countries, running under the Black Sea, which started supplying gas in 2003 (its construction was strongly opposed by the United States because it would undermine the commercial viability of pipeline projects that Washington supported). Russia and Turkey are now discussing the possibility of additional energy deals, including the possibility at some juncture of Turkey's re-exporting Russian gas to Europe, which would expand Turkey's role as a transit country for fuel beyond Caspian oil and gas. The relationship is not just fueled by gas, however. Turkish construction and consumer-goods companies such as Enka, Alarko, and Anadolu have major ventures in Russia. Furthermore, Turkey was the top destination for Russian tourists in 2006, with nearly 2 million Russian visitors, the largest number from any country except Germany.

Paradoxically, even Turkey's European vocation has brought it closer to Russia, for both countries are frustrated with the EU, which they feel treats them as second-tier states. Both instead want the European Union to recognize and respect them as European great powers, with significant imperial histories and roles in the Near East and Eurasia. In many respects, Russia and Turkey are undergoing parallel revivals of their imperial state traditions.

Iran

Much to the dismay of the United States, and even of some of its European allies, Turkey has also been strengthening its relationship with Iran. The rapprochement between the two long-standing geopolitical rivals has been driven by two factors: a common interest in combating Kurdish separatism and Turkey's rapidly growing energy needs.

The most important factor in bringing Turkey and Iran together has been a joint determination to prevent the emergence of an independent Kurdish state, which would likely be composed of not only Iraqi but potentially also Turkish and Iranian territory. Just as Turkey has been facing increasing attacks from the PKK, Iran has been fighting against is own rebellious Kurdish group, the Party for Free Life in Kurdistan (Partiya Jiyana Azada Kurdistane—PJAK), itself affiliated with the PKK. Although Turkey and Iran have not undertaken any joint military operations against the two groups, they have shared intelligence on the common threat, and each has arrested fighters from both organizations. Iran has detained and extradited to Turkey a number of PKK militants, and Iran and Turkey have both carried out air strikes against PKK and PJAK positions in the Kandil Mountains of northern Iraq.[6] Iran's ambassador in Ankara, Firouz Dolatabadi, has called for Turkey, Iran, and Syria to adopt a joint position on the Kurdish issue, lest "the U.S. carve pieces from us for a Kurdish state."[7] Iran's aim seems to be not only to pursue its own security interests vis-à-vis the Kurds, but to lure Turkey away from its traditional Western orientation.

Iran has also been using its considerable energy leverage for that same purpose. Iran is the second largest supplier of natural gas to Turkey (after Russia), and energy ties between Turkey and Iran are increasing. Already, in 1996, then Turkish Prime Minister Erbakan concluded a $23 billion deal for the delivery of natural gas from Iran over twenty-five years. Even after Erbakan's ouster, none of his secular successors abandoned that deal, and in 2001 Turkey signed a further agreement with Iran to open a gas pipeline running from the Iranian city of Tabriz to Ankara.

Notwithstanding American pressure on Turkey to shun Iran and instead import and transport gas from Central Asia through the Caspian Sea, Turkey under Erdogan has continued to increase energy imports from Iran. In February 2007 it signed two energy deals, one to allow the Turkish Petroleum Corporation to explore oil and natural gas in Iran and another for the transfer of gas through a pipeline in Iran from Turkmenistan to Turkey, and then on to Europe.[8] In July 2007 Turkey and Iran signed a further memorandum of understanding allowing the Turkish Petroleum Corporation to produce 20 billion cubic meters of natural gas in three sections of Iran's massive South Pars gas field.[9] Turkish energy officials estimate that the project will require a total investment of around $3.5 billion, including approximately $2 billion to build a pipeline to transport the gas across Turkey.

Since the AKP came to power in November 2002, Turkey's economic relationship with Iran has expanded even beyond the major gas and pipeline deals. In 2006 bilateral trade between the two countries reached $6.7 billion, an increase of 52.5 percent over 2005 and more than five times the level of $1.2 billion in 2002. The growth in bilateral trade between Turkey and Iran appears to be part of the AKP's strategy of trying to strengthen economic ties with other Muslim countries. In summer 2007, Foreign Trade Minister Kursad Tuzmen announced that Turkey would soon sign preferential trade agreements with 18 Islamic countries including Iran and Pakistan.[10] He said that tariff barriers between the countries would be reduced in stages as part of an attempt to boost trade among the ten members of the Economic Cooperation Organization (ECO), which includes Turkey, Iran, Pakistan, Afghanistan, and the six Central Asian republics. In addition to further antagonizing Washington, any attempt to grant preferential trade status to Iran and Pakistan could create problems for Turkey in its relations with the EU, which is Turkey's main export market. Under the terms of Turkey's 1995 Customs Union Agreement with the EU, which came into force on January 1, 1996, all of Turkey's tariff barriers with third parties must be harmonized with those of the EU.

Neither the tactical cooperation on the Kurdish issue nor the expanding energy relationship mean that Turkey somehow thinks a relationship with Iran can replace its traditional relationship with the West. Among other issues, Shi'a Iran's apparent pursuit of a nuclear weapons capability is seen in Sunni Turkey as a major challenge, which could even lead Turkey to reexamine its own non-nuclear status at some point in the future. Still, for most Turks, the option of closer ties with Iran can be used to balance the relationship with a West that is no longer trusted or admired in Turkey as it once was. The hypothetical threat of a nuclear Iran, moreover, is considered modest next to the reality of the threat of Kurdish separatism. On that issue, at least, Turks see Iran as a more reliable ally than the United States.

Syria

Turkey has also been increasing cooperation with its longtime foe Syria for many of the same reasons it is reassessing its relationship with Iran. During the 1980s and 1990s, when Turkey's war with the PKK was at its peak, Syria provided the PKK a safe haven in part as leverage over Turkey in the two countries' serious disputes over water. Syria had complained that Turkey's Southeastern Anatolia Project (Guneydogu Anadolu Projesi—GAP), an enormous series of dams and other irrigation and infrastructure projects in southeastern Turkey, was denying Syria access to badly needed water supplies by preventing the water from reaching it. Turkey's response to Syrian support for the PKK was to initiate strategic cooperation with Syria's enemy Israel, which culminated in an extensive military and intelligence cooperation agreement with Prime Minister Benjamin Netanyahu in 1996.

Syrian leader Hafez al-Asad's decision to expel the PKK leader Abdullah Ocalan in 1998, in response to a Turkish military threat, paved the way for a gradual improvement in economic and diplomatic relations between Ankara and Damascus. As with Iran, the main driver of the Turkish-Syrian rapprochement is the common interest in dealing with Kurdish separatists. Both Ankara and Damascus worry that the Iraq War has unleashed a serious threat of Kurdish nationalism that both must work together to contain. In part to demonstrate this new willingness to work together on this common challenge, in January 2005 Syrian President Bashar al-Asad traveled to Ankara for the first trip by a Syrian president to Turkey since Syria's independence in 1946.[11]

Also as with Iran, Syria seeks to use the rapprochement with Turkey to break free of the isolation the West has imposed on it since the assassination of Lebanese Prime Minister Rafik Hariri in February 2005. It has done so in part by developing its economic relationship with Turkey. Between 2005 and 2007, Syrian authorities have approved more than thirty Turkish investment projects in the country with a total value of over $150 million. Bilateral trade is expected to be around $1.5 billion in 2007, more than triple the figure when the AKP came to power in November 2002. An agreement was reached for the establishment of a free-trade zone in 2006, and with Damascus encouraging Turkish investment the two countries have established a joint company for oil exploration. The number of Turkish tourists to Syria increased from almost nothing in the late 1990s to nearly 250,000 in 2007.[12]

Although the United States has pressed Turkey not to deal with the Syrian regime, Turkey seeks a more independent role, as it does in its relations with Lebanon and Palestine. It has repeatedly offered its good offices to broker Syrian-Israeli dialogue to both

Washington and Tel Aviv.[13] Such Turkish efforts paid off in May 2008, when Israeli and Syrian officials began indirect negotiations in Istanbul through the mediation of a Turkish delegation led by Ahmet Davutoglu.[14]

Where does all this new regional activism of Turkey's lead? Two distinct scenarios seem possible. In one, the AKP government continues on its current course, developing its ties with other regional actors while seeking to maintain a close alliance with the United States and a viable candidacy for membership in the European Union. This hardly means differences and tensions with the West would be avoided, as the last few years have certainly shown, but it need not lead to the West's "losing" Turkey, either, whatever the ongoing differences with the West over Iraq, the Kurds, and other issues.

There is, however, another potential scenario for a Turkish split with the West, one that is far more dramatic and, though unlikely, not to be ruled out, given Turkey's growing domestic political divide: a coup against the AKP government. In the event of a military, or even judicial, intervention against the AKP, Turkey could move in an isolationist, authoritarian direction that could put it in more direct opposition to Europe and even the United States. After all, the hard-line elements in Turkey's Kemalist establishment believe the United States and Europe are helping to erode Turkey's secular identity by promoting "moderate Islam" and are convinced that the West supports an independent Kurdish state in Iraq.[15] In the event of such a coup, the military, unlike its 1997 intervention against the anti-Western Islamists under Erbakan, this time would be acting against a popular, democratically elected government that had set its sights on joining the EU. Such a coup would all but end EU membership prospects (which could, in fact, be one of the objectives of those undertaking such a coup). In light of the troubled relations with Washington because of the Kurdish question, Turkey's post-coup authoritarian leaders might well break with the West and seek closer ties with authoritarian states such as Russia, China, Syria, Iran, Azerbaijan, and the Central Asian republics. That Eurasian alternative, sometimes expressed openly by retired generals, would also enable Ankara to take action against the Kurds without worrying about the reaction from the liberal West. This scenario remains unlikely—but as domestic tensions rise in Turkey, it would be naive to exclude it. It would certainly qualify as the "loss" of Turkey.

CHAPTER SIX

Winning Turkey

TURKEY IS NOT "lost," but it could be unless recent trends are reversed and Turks are given a reason to believe, as they have for more than eighty years, that their future is best assured as part of the Western world. How can Turkey's Western and democratic orientation be preserved? What can the United States and Europe do to overcome the growing estrangement between themselves and Turkey? What can Turkey itself do?

There are many possible answers to these questions, and a comprehensive agenda on the full set of issues is beyond the scope of this short book. But here are five important steps the United States, Europe, and Turkey can take to help put Turkey's relationship with the West back on course.

1. Promote a "Grand Bargain" between Turkey and the Kurds

The place to start is with the Kurdish issue, which threatens Turkey's stability and confidence in the West more than any other. The United States cannot take back the invasion of Iraq, which most Turks blame for the flare-up in PKK violence, but there are a number of steps it could take to minimize the Turkish perception that Americans do not take Turkish interests into account. The most critical measures include greater U.S. support for limited Turkish military action against the PKK; the exercise of American leverage over the Iraqi Kurds; support for the political and cultural rights of Kurds in Turkey; and the promotion of a mutually beneficial "grand bargain" between Turkey and the Kurds of northern Iraq.

American reluctance to support Turkish military action against the PKK in Iraq is understandable; northern Iraq has been one of the few stable parts of the country, and the last thing American military commanders there want to do is open a new front in the Iraq conflict. As one senior U.S. official recently put it, "If you're a Turkey hand, you say, 'For crying out loud, why isn't CENTCOM taking action?' If you're looking at it from Iraq, you say, 'Hey, we've got our hands full; let's not stir the nest up.'"[1] The roots of Turkey's problem with Kurdish terrorism are primarily internal, and attacking Kurdish militants in Iraq could provoke the PKK to launch even more domestic terror attacks.

At the same time, America's failure to act militarily against the PKK and its opposition to Turkey's doing so have been among the most important causes of Turkey's growing disenchantment with the West. When the U.S. commander in charge of northern Iraq, General Benjamin R. Mixon, was asked in October 2007 why Turkey considers the PKK such a serious threat, Mixon responded, "I have no idea. You'll have to ask Turkey."[2] Such apparent U.S. indifference to murderous cross-border terrorist attacks on Turkey leaves the United States open to charges that it cares only about terrorists who attack Americans, undercuts American leverage against the Iraqi Kurds, and contributes to the feeling in

Ankara that Turkey must act unilaterally, which could trigger a disastrous confrontation with Kurdish Peshmerga forces.

Worried about the consequences of such a unilateral intervention, the United States has since late 2007 been taking a stronger line against the PKK, both by backing limited Turkish military action and by providing more intelligence to the Turks. Such American support is a step in the right direction and has helped strengthen the Turkish public's severely shaken trust in the United States. It could be usefully bolstered by Washington's own efforts to kill or arrest known PKK leaders and pressure on Europeans to crack down on PKK financing. Such actions would help demonstrate the United States' seriousness of purpose by matching its words about fighting terrorism with deeds, and also help take pressure off the government in Ankara for a more comprehensive, and likely counterproductive, ground invasion. Washington needs to reassure Turks that it is concerned with the terrorists who attack Turkey, not just those who attack the United States.

In reality there is no military solution to the PKK problem, and Turkish or U.S. military action must be limited to the goal of striking unambiguous terrorist targets and putting pressure on Kurdish leaders to rein in the threat of terrorism, while avoiding civilian casualties to the maximum extent possible. It is a fine line for the United States to tread, but also an issue that it cannot avoid. The United States must continue to develop a close relationship with Iraqi Kurds and to support their aspirations for autonomy within Iraq, but also make clear that formal independence, support for irredentism, tolerance of terrorism, or repression of minority rights will cost them American support. It is true that the United States needs a good relationship with its Kurdish partners, but the Kurds need a good relationship with the United States even more, and Washington must use whatever leverage it has.

To complement its solidarity with Turkey on the terrorism issue, the United States should also continue to encourage Ankara to move forward with efforts to guarantee greater cultural rights for its own Kurdish population. Ultimately, the Kurdish problem will only be solved when Turkey's 15 million to 20 million Kurdish citizens feel fully represented and at home in the Turkish Republic. The Erdogan government has recognized this essential point and undertaken limited efforts to enhance Kurdish language and cultural rights and to promote economic development in southeastern Turkey. In 2003 the AKP government overcame then President Ahmet Necdet Sezer's veto to pass a series of reforms, including the right to broadcast in the Kurdish language, the right to give children Kurdish names, and the elimination of a law banning "separatist propaganda" that had often been used as a pretext to detain thousands of Kurdish intellectuals and activists.[3]

In an important speech in Diyarbakir in August 2005, Erdogan acknowledged past "mistakes" in dealing with the Kurdish problem and insisted that "democracy," not repression, was the solution.[4] President Gul also argues that it was a mistake to ban the Kurdish language and that although Kurds should learn Turkish, they have a right to preserve their native language as well. Such rhetorical openings have created high expectations among the Kurdish masses, but they remain largely unfulfilled. Although the AKP passed more democratic legislation than most previous Turkish governments, the record on implementation and effectiveness is mixed. For instance, the use of the Kurdish language in Turkish radio and television and public education is still strictly limited and in some cases simply illegal. Even the symbolic use of the Kurdish language at the local administration level—or even, for example, its use by private citizens in greeting cards—is subject to prosecution by national authorities.

The AKP has opposed judicial attempts to close down Kurdish political parties, with Erdogan arguing that Turkey "should not choose antidemocratic means against those who have entered parliament with the votes of hundreds of thousands of our citizens."[5] He argues that if Kurds are prevented from participating in the political process they are more likely to be driven into the arms of the PKK. There are also some signs that the AKP is considering a partial amnesty law that would be designed to encourage PKK members to reject violence and pursue their political aims peacefully.[6] Previous amnesty laws that have given amnesty only to those who have provided information on the PKK and have themselves committed no violent crimes have not been effective in weakening the organization, but some mechanism for exempting former rebels from prosecution if they genuinely renounce violence will likely be necessary if Turkey is to integrate them peacefully back into society. Yet the issue remains extremely controversial in the eyes of hard-liners within the Turkish military. Nationalist elements within the AKP are equally reluctant to be portrayed as "soft" on Turkey's foremost national security issue, while President Gul and Prime Minister Erdogan have made it clear that they agree with the Turkish military on the need to stand firmly against any kind of compromise with the PKK.

The PKK, of course, is unlikely to give up its tactics. Even if there were major democratic openings from Ankara, it remains doubtful that the PKK would lay down its arms. On the contrary, hard-liners within the PKK can be expected to do everything in their power to thwart such measures, including using violence to provoke the Turkish state toward repression that it believes will swell PKK ranks—a trap that Ankara must do all it can to avoid. Fortunately,

there are signs that even many in the Turkish military, long proponents of a hard-line repression of the rebellion and skeptical of
political outreach, realize this. According to *Generals' Front*, a book
by journalist Fikret Bila, consisting of interviews with Turkey's
most recent military leaders, most of the generals concluded that
Turkey's reliance on force to repress the Kurds had only played into
the hands of the PKK. The book was excerpted in the Turkish daily
Milliyet in November 2007, which would have been unlikely had
the Turkish General Staff opposed its message.[7] Even the hard-line
chief of the Turkish General Staff, General Mehmet Yasar
Buyukanit, agrees that "the fight against terrorism calls for not only
military but also economic, cultural and social measures."[8]

Finally, the United States should seek to sponsor a direct relationship between Turkey and Iraqi Kurdish leaders, with the ultimate goal of striking a mutually beneficial "grand bargain"
between these longs-standing rivals. While such an agreement
may seem improbable in the current atmosphere, in which
Turkey conducts periodic military operations in northern Iraq
and Turkish troops are poised on the border, the basis for a grand
bargain is that the interests of key parties are in fact aligned. Iraqi
Kurds need Turkish investment, trade, and cooperation in the
energy field. According to Henri Barkey, a proponent of the grand
bargain, the 1,200 Turkish companies operating in northern Iraq
have generated some $2 billion in business, an amount that could
rise considerably if Turkish companies were able to win some of
the more than $15 billion in contracts that the Kurdish Regional
Government is likely to issue in the next three years.[9]

Moreover, Iraqi Kurds must understand that their region cannot prosper under the ongoing threat of Turkish invasion. Turkey,
meanwhile, has an interest in a stable and prosperous secular
neighbor where minority rights for the local Turkmen population are upheld. Iraqi Kurdish leaders will have an interest in

shutting down the PKK if they understand that failure to do so will scuttle their own aspirations for autonomy and that the rights of Turkish Kurds are protected in Turkey. Some Turks fear that a prosperous "Kurdistan" within Iraq increases the chances that Turkey's own Kurds will pursue a violent fight for independence, but the opposite is in fact more likely. A recognized, autonomous Kurdish region in Iraq that enjoys good relations with Ankara would know that it would have much to lose by threatening the integrity of its stronger northern neighbor.

For any of this to happen, the United States needs to take the lead. It should encourage the leaders of Turkey and the Kurdish Regional Government to meet, under U.S. or UN auspices, with the aim of a reaching comprehensive and binding agreements on the status of the ethnically mixed city of Kirkuk (the December 2007 agreement to postpone a referendum on Kirkuk's status buys time to negotiate a special arrangement); recognized borders; the Yumurtalik pipeline; joint border patrols; and trade and investment relations. Such a comprehensive grand bargain will hardly be easy, but the AKP's strong democratic backing in the aftermath of the July 22, 2007, elections—and increased credibility with the Turkish military following the December 2007 military actions—give them at least a chance to pull it off. In the event of the AKP's closure by the Turkish judiciary, especially at a time when a similar fate could await the Kurdish nationalist party in parliament, Turkey's disenfranchised Kurds could lose faith in the democratic process. Such an outcome would also end hopes of a grand bargain between Turkey and the Iraqi Kurds.

2. Support Liberalism and Democracy in Turkey

The United States can best help anchor Turkey in the West by standing steadfastly for democracy and liberalism in Turkey. In a highly polarized Turkish political situation, the United States should not play favorites but instead should make clear that it will work with any democratically elected government that respects individual freedom and the rule of law. Although it is always tempting for the United States to side reflexively with traditional strategic allies in the Turkish establishment and to oppose political parties with Islamic roots, Washington must be careful to avoid giving the impression that it will do so at the expense of the popular will in Turkey, thereby alienating potential pro-Western allies. So long as an Islamic-oriented government does not seek to impose a religious agenda on secular Turks, and especially if it maintains a strong pro-Western and democratic orientation, there is no reason for the United States and Europe not to support it.

The United States initially failed to meet this standard when the Turkish General Staff sought to interfere in the political process in the spring of 2007. In the days following the April 27 "e-coup," Washington did not clearly stand up for the principle of democratic rule—despite calls by the elected Turkish government to do so—and simply noted, "We don't take sides."[10] While Washington remained mum, the European Union enlargement commissioner, Olli Rehn, made it clear that the military's intervention was "a clear test case whether the Turkish armed forces respect democratic secularization and democratic values." On May 1, Secretary of State Condoleezza Rice finally noted that "the United States fully supports Turkish democracy and its constitutional processes, and that means that the election, the electoral system and the results of the electoral system and the results of the constitutional process have to be upheld."[11]

The United States also failed to react vigorously to the chief prosecutor's March 2008 case for banning the AKP. Whereas EU Commissioner Rehn warned that shutting down the AKP would jeopardize Turkey's EU talks and the EU high representative for foreign policy, Javier Solana, warned that "the consequences would be very grave," Rice again failed to take a stand, noting only that the case was "a matter . . . for Turks to decide."[12] Washington understandably does not want to get caught up in internal Turkish disputes, but clearer articulation of U.S. opposition to what would effectively be a judicial coup would help to avoid alienating a large portion of the Turkish population and put the military on notice that it will not get a free pass from Washington to interfere in the democratic process. Failure to do so could inadvertently give a green light to a military intervention (or a military-backed judicial intervention) that would alienate more than half of Turkey's citizens and potentially end its hopes of joining the EU.

The Turkish establishment's concerns about Islamism are legitimate; Turkey's secular traditions should be protected, and worries about fundamentalism are not the result of mere paranoia. But it is also important not to exaggerate the Islamist threat or to confuse the AKP with previous Islamist groups, and it is critical not to take potentially counterproductive steps to neutralize it. After all, the AKP, in power since 2002, has done little to suggest a desire to impose an Islamist agenda. It has respected the rights of secular Turks and earned a reputation for managerial competence and a commitment to democracy that had eluded its recent predecessors, contributing to its becoming the first Turkish government in over fifty years to be reelected with a larger share of the votes than the last time. In the run-up to the 2007 elections, it replaced over 150 members of parliament with new candidates from all spheres of society to demonstrate its transformation from an Islamic-oriented party to a more modern, "catch-all," centrist party.[13] In early 2008, Erdogan's promotion of legislation making it possible for women to wear Islamic headscarves at universities and the perception that he was acting to favor the economic interests of his conservative allies caused concern among many secular Turks who felt he was not delivering on his postelection commitment to reassure them. Still, the AKP leadership seems to realize that it would be the first victim of any effort to impose Islamism on an unwilling Turkish public. Having avoided the fate of his party's closure in summer 2008, Erdogan has a new opportunity to demonstrate his commitment to Turkey's secular principles and to try to govern with as broad a social consensus as possible.

Even beyond AKP's track record there are other reasons to have confidence that democracy in Turkey will not produce an Islamic state. One is a deeply rooted secular state tradition that predates Kemalism. The Ottoman Empire was itself hardly a theocracy, thanks to a body of laws promulgated outside the realm of sharia law. This legacy stands in contrast to the situation in the Arab world, Iran, and postcolonial formations such as Malaysia or Indonesia, where the state is a product of Islam and Islam was needed for the state to earn political legitimacy.

Second, tolerant, liberal democracy is arguably the best antidote to radical Islam. In the absence of free political expression, the mosque becomes the only outlet for dissent and Islam the only voice of resistance against tyranny. People who compare Iran and Turkey forget that Iran under the shah was an authoritarian dictatorship, just like most of the Arab world today. In the absence of liberal democracy, Islam becomes a panacea. "Islam is the solution" is the motto of the Muslim Brotherhood, the most powerful political movement in the Arab world. Turkey managed to avoid inadvertently fostering radical Islamism by becoming a democracy in 1946. But if Turkey were to emulate the Arab world and abolish democratic rule in the name of strengthening secularism, the long-term result would likely be a strengthening of radical Islam.

Finally, Turkey is likely to remain averse to Islamic rule because it has a vibrant new middle class that greatly benefits from capitalism, democracy, and globalization. Turkey should in some ways be thankful for not having vast oil and gas resources. Energy abundance can be a curse that paralyzes prospects for democracy and capitalism in the Middle East. Instead, the Turkish economy is fueled by productivity and export-oriented "Anatolian tigers." Turkey's devout entrepreneurs dream about the EU and maximizing their profits, not about an Islamic revolution.

In the wake of the strong electoral mandate the new AKP government received in July 2007, it has an opportunity to consolidate liberalism and democracy in Turkey in a way that should not threaten the secular establishment. The AKP is rightly pursuing the promulgation of a new constitution to replace the 1982 constitution written under military rule. A new constitution could provide for greater individual freedoms, more opportunity for women and minorities, and more democratic institutions. It will be critically important, however, to ensure that the new constitution ultimately is drafted by a broad-based constitutional council rather than by a group of party-friendly hand-picked professors, an approach that would risk merely replacing the "military constitution" with the "AKP constitution" and undermining the legitimacy of the new system.[14]

Strengthening democracy also requires Turkey to further amend or abolish Article 301 of the penal code, which prohibits insults to the Turkish nation and state institutions and severely restricts freedom of speech in Turkey. It has been used more than sixty times in the past few years, often to prosecute intellectuals and dissidents, including Nobel Prize–winning novelist Orhan Pamuk (for talking about the massacres of Armenians during World War I); the slain journalist Hrant Dink (for claiming that those massacres amounted to "genocide"); and Joost Lagendijk, a supporter of Turkish EU membership and chairman of the EU-Turkey Joint Parliamentary Committee (for comments critical of the Turkish military's actions in the conflict with the PKK). In April 2008, the Turkish parliament approved a government-backed proposal to amend the article, reducing the maximum sentence for denigrating Turkish identity or institutions from three years to two and replacing the vaguely defined crime of denigrating "Turkishness" with the somewhat more specific ban on denigrating the "Turkish nation."[15] Still, most observers agree that even the revised article provides plenty of scope for abuse, and the new version is unlikely to constrain aggressive prosecutors. President Gul admitted before the modification of its wording that Article 301 "damages Turkey's image" and is seen as a "ban on freedom of expression and thought."[16] Repealing it not only would make Turkey a freer place but also would enhance its image in the eyes of the West.

In dealing with such controversial issues, including also the sensitive question of allowing Turkish women to wear headscarves at universities, AKP leaders will have to proceed cautiously, and consult with a full cross-section of Turkish society to try to build a national consensus for change. If the government can win broad support for a new constitution, Turkey will emerge as a more liberal and democratic state, better placed for membership in the European Union and to maintain close relations with the United States.

3. Renew Commitment to Turkey's Membership in the EU

The growing Turkish impression that the European Union will never accept Turkey as a full member has been deeply damaging. It has led to increasing Turkish mistrust of the West and to a strong perception among many Turks that Turkey must seek other global partnerships as an alternative to an "anti-Muslim" EU. To allow this perception to develop further or, worse, to confirm it by excluding the possibility of Turkish membership in the EU by replacing it with a "privileged partnership" would be counterproductive.

The incentive of EU membership has led to major political, economic, social, legal, and diplomatic reforms that are in the interest of Turkey and the West alike. These reforms have helped contribute to unprecedented economic growth, a freer society, stronger Turkish democracy, and more flexibility on tough foreign policy questions such as Cyprus. After decades of telling Turkey it is eligible in principle to join the EU, it would be catastrophic now to tell it that membership is excluded regardless of what it does. Already, many Turks are starting to ask why they should continue to do difficult things to qualify for inclusion in the EU when all the signals coming from Europe are that the EU is closing its doors to Turkey no matter what they do. Turks know that in the best of circumstances it will probably be a decade before their full membership is realistic. But by 2018 the EU will be a very different place, and so will Turkey. The EU could help alleviate some of Turkey's growing resentment of the West by reiterating and finding a way to demonstrate that its goal remains full Turkish membership, so long as the established criteria are met.

The best way to handle this difficult issue in the meantime would be for EU leaders to take immediate steps to bring Turkey closer to the EU in concrete ways while reiterating the goal of full membership when all the criteria are met. The objective of this initiative would be to improve relations and deepen ties between Turkey and the EU in the short term while encouraging full membership over time.

Specifically, a renewed set of mutual commitments between Turkey and the EU could include the following elements:

—The addition of agriculture and services to the Turkey-EU customs union, which would boost and help to modernize the Turkish economy

—Annual meetings between the EU foreign policy chief and the Turkish foreign minister for discussions of regional and global foreign and security policy issues

—A special Turkish role in the European Security and Defense Policy (ESDP), which could include Turkish contributions to the newly created EU "battle groups" and inclusion in the EU Rapid Reaction Force. Such military cooperation could help demonstrate to EU member states that have undermanned and underfunded military forces the potential of having a member with a large and capable army.

—Enhanced EU financial support for Turkey's Southeast, designed to promote the sort of economic growth and job creation that can help integrate Turkey's Kurdish citizens and help Turkey meet the EU's membership criteria

—Special visa provisions for Turks with qualifying educational backgrounds

—Exchange programs for Turkish diplomats and military officers with their European counterparts

—Expansion of educational and civil-society exchange programs, to be jointly funded by Turkey and the EU

—An EU-Turkey "energy dialogue" on issues of long-term mutual concern, including pipelines, tanker traffic in the Bosphorus, environmental issues, and energy relations with key players such as Iran and Russia

—EU outreach teams from member states, including new members with fresh experience with the accession process, to help explain to Turkish partners how the EU works

These and other potential measures would complement, not replace, the ongoing accession process, with its lengthy, detailed, chapter-by-chapter review of Turkish readiness for membership. Their purpose would be to provide mechanisms to accelerate that process and to demonstrate concretely to skeptical Turks that a lengthy accession process does not necessarily mean an endless one.

If the EU upholds its obligations and takes steps such as these to bring Turkey closer, Turks should understand that the accession process will indeed take time and that the only real path to membership is in persuading European publics that Turkish membership is in their interest. Ultimately, Turkey can neither sneak into the EU unnoticed nor bully its way in. In the past Turkey has sometimes argued that its democracy is so fragile that rejection by the EU could lead to political instability—not a particularly compelling selling point. Similarly, some in Turkey have tried to reassure Europeans that there is no need to worry about Islamism because the generals will never permit it; again a strange case to make in an effort to join a democratic union. Instead, Turkey needs to demonstrate that it is evolving into a highly stable, liberal, prosperous, and strong democracy, and that the EU membership path bolsters that evolution. Turkish membership must be sold not as a threat but an asset.

Turkey will also need to accept that European doubts about Turkish membership are legitimate and not some form of racism. Accepting such a large new member, whose population of over 70 million would give it a large role in EU decisionmaking institutions, is a major step that cannot be taken lightly. Consequently, if arrangements such as a temporary "emergency brake" provision on free movement of Turkish labor are seen as a prerequisite to reassure European opinion that the EU will not be flooded by poor and difficult-to-assimilate workers, then such provisions might have to be accepted as the price of joining the club. The East European countries who joined the EU in 2004 did not like the fact that most existing members did not immediately allow immigration from those countries, but they accepted it and have benefited immensely as a result. By 2020, the demographically challenged EU might be in such need of low-wage laborers that member states will be seeking immigration from a by then more advanced, democratic and prosperous Turkey rather than trying to prevent it.

Everybody, including the Turks, realizes that the path will be difficult and that accession cannot happen anytime soon. But those European leaders who had the strategic vision to promote Turkey's candidacy in the first place need to continue to make the case that a democratic, prosperous, and strong Turkey within the EU is in Europe's own self-interest. Having come this far with Turkey over the decades, for the EU to allow the membership bid to fail now could end up having worse consequences than if the process had never gotten started.

4. Promote Historic Compromise with Armenia

Turkey's growing alienation from the West has also been exacerbated by its strained relationship with the Republic of Armenia, and in particular by initiatives in Europe and the United States to accuse Turkey of genocide for the massacre during World War I of ethnic Armenians then living within the territory of the Ottoman Empire. The success of such measures in the form of legislative action to officially recognize genocide would further alienate and anger Turkey, undermine efforts to promote reconciliation between Turkey and Armenia, and exacerbate Turkish nationalism. An alternative approach to this difficult set of issues would be for the West to press Turkey to repair its relations with the Republic of Armenia and to allow open debate within Turkey. A Turkey that itself moved to shed greater light on these historical events and allowed open discussion about them would be a more welcome member of the West, would stand a better chance of reconciliation with Armenia and the Armenian diaspora, would improve Turkey's chances of getting into the EU, and would undercut the efforts of Armenian extremists to isolate Turkey.

As a first step, U.S. and European leaders should accelerate diplomatic efforts to resolve the bilateral conflict between Turkey and the Republic of Armenia, which has for so long blocked peaceful developments in the Caucasus and complicates Turkey's accession to the EU. When the Soviet Union broke up in 1989, the former Soviet Republic of Armenia occupied Nagorno-Karabakh, an ethnic Armenian enclave within Azerbaijan. This led Turkey to break relations with Armenia and declare a blockade of the landlocked republic.

Progress on the issue of Nagorno-Karabakh could provide an opportunity for a major breakthrough across a range of areas. In 2006 France, Russia, and the United States—the co-chairs of the Minsk Group (an organization formed to resolve the Armenia-Azerbaijan conflict—proposed the following guidelines for a settlement:[17]

—Renunciation of the use of force

—Armenian withdrawal from areas of Azerbaijan surrounding Nagorno-Karabakh that they have occupied

—An interim status for Nagorno-Karabakh, with substantial international aid, including peacekeepers

—Mutual commitment to a referendum on Nagorno-Karabakh's final status after the return of displaced Azeris[18]

The United States should encourage Turkey to pledge now that if Armenia shows a real commitment to a solution to the Nagorno-

Karabakh conflict, Turkey would reestablish diplomatic relations with Armenia, end its blockade, and open the land border between the two countries. Such steps not only would be in the interest of both countries but also could create the climate for a long-term solution in Nagorno-Karabakh as well as much better relations and open trade between Turkey, Armenia, and Azerbaijan.

Even more important is to find a new way of handling the historical disputes between Turks and Armenians. Recent legislative efforts to recognize that tragedy officially as genocide in France, the European parliament, and the U.S. Congress have provoked strong Turkish reactions.[19] Even liberal Turks, who acknowledge that atrocities were committed, have trouble understanding why foreign legislatures should be determining how to characterize the actions of their Ottoman predecessors more than ninety years ago. As a practical matter, the costs to the West of foreigners' pressing for Turkey's capitulation on this issue in terms of Turkey's predictably negative reaction almost certainly outweigh any gains to be had.

Although such a sensitive matter must obviously be handled by the Turks and Armenians themselves, their American and European friends should actively encourage a solution, which should begin with Turkey's allowing more open research and debate about the subject. Turkey's contention that "history should be left to the historians" is fine as far as it goes, but it would be more convincing if Turkey actually did that, rather than prosecute historians and others who reach the conclusion that genocide took place. This is another reason why Article 301 should be repealed.

The Turkish government's proposal for a joint commission to study the events of 1915 was a positive first step. Still, the Erdogan government needs to be more vocal in its support for freedom of speech on the Armenian question. In 2005 the then justice minister of the AKP government blamed the organizers of a conference on the Armenian question for "stabbing the Turkish nation in the back."[20] Originally planned to take place at Bosphorus University, the event had to be canceled and was later held under strict police protection at the private Bilgi University, where it nonetheless came under assault from nationalists.

It is also time for the Turkish government to take more constructive and creative steps toward political and psychological reconciliation with Armenia. Ankara has a tendency to see the genocide issue either as a historic dispute that should be discussed among historians or as a legal problem, which needs to be analyzed in the framework of international law and the exact legal definition of genocide. Neither of these two approaches can address the human dimension of the tragedy. Ankara and the Turkish public need to understand better the trauma of 1915 for the Armenian people and the Armenian diaspora.

An olive branch to Armenia in the form of a presidential letter of sympathy to commemorate the tragedy would help to bring a human dimension to relations between Ankara and Yerevan, the capital of Armenia. The United States should stand with Turks who want to make further progress on the issue, including some who propose building a monument to all the Turks and Armenians who lost their lives in World War I. The Turkish government should issue a statement that the Republic of Turkey acknowledges that atrocities were committed, regrets the events of that tragic period, and deplores the suffering and loss of life on both sides. It may not satisfy everyone, but it would go some way toward showing sensitivity to the need to accept Turkey's past and pave the way to better ties with Armenia, Europe, and the United States. One stumbling block to Turkey's issuing such a statement is its serious concern that any step toward acknowledging genocide would trigger Armenian territorial and financial demands for compensation. Some indication from Armenia that this would not take place could greatly alleviate Turkey's concerns and help Turkey come to terms with painful chapters of its history with more self-confidence.

Finally, Turkey and Armenia should work together on student and journalist exchange programs. Jointly established "Hrant Dink" chairs in an Armenian and Turkish university could become a meaningful way to launch and promote such dialogue. Ultimately, real progress toward mutual understanding will come only thanks to human contact and genuine attempts at transcending each others' "nationalist narrative."

5. Promote a Political Settlement in Cyprus

The perception of Western unfairness on the Cyprus issue has also contributed to Turkey's alienation from the West. Many Turks believe that their politically difficult efforts to promote a political settlement on the island were not reciprocated by the Greek Cypriots, and that Europe and the United States have not lived up to their promises to reward the Turkish Cypriots for their willingness to compromise. There is some evidence to support this view. The Turkish government and the Turkish Cypriots made painful political compromises in order to achieve a political settlement and improve Turkey's EU prospects, but the Greek Cypriots voted against that settlement. Nevertheless, they were rewarded with EU membership, while Turkish Cypriots got little. The United States and the European Union did not fulfill their promises to lessen the isolation of northern Cyprus, and Turkey's EU prospects are now in Nicosia's hands.

The best outcome for Cyprus remains an eventual political settlement based on principles like those proposed in the Annan Plan. Prospects for such a settlement had been dim since the

Annan Plan failed, but they improved significantly in February 2008, when the moderate Communist Party leader, Demetris Christofias, defeated the hard-line Greek Cypriot nationalist, Tassos Papadopoulos, in Cyprus's presidential election. Christofias immediately reached out to the leader of the Turkish Cypriots, Mehmet Ali Talat—an old colleague from the pan-Cypriot trade union movement—and agreed to move forward with political negotiations. In April 2008 the United Nations for the first time in several years began preparatory work to pave the way for peace talks, and the two sides agreed to the highly symbolic opening of the Ledra Street crossing in Nicosia. The two sides remain far apart on the issues that have divided them for decades, but the goodwill of the leaders provides the best opportunity for a political settlement that Cyprus has seen since the Annan Plan was rejected.[21] Americans and Europeans should intensify their efforts to promote such a settlement.

A comprehensive settlement of the Cyprus issue on the basis of a federation that split Cyprus into largely autonomous zones for the two ethnic communities (a "bi-zonal, bi-communal" federation, in the UN jargon) would benefit all sides. Greek Cypriots would get back more territory, see the departure of most or all Turkish troops from the island, benefit from trade with Turkey's vibrant economy, and finally receive compensation for families displaced from their homes in 1974. In turn, Turkish Cypriots would become full EU citizens, escape from the political and economic isolation under which they've suffered for years, and increase the prospects that one day Turkey itself would join the EU.[22] If U.S. or EU leadership can help the parties reach a compromise solution, no effort should be spared to do so.

In the name of reaching such a solution, Turkey should be prepared—and the United States and Europe should encourage it—to undertake goodwill gestures to signal its determination to reach an agreement. For example, without any risk to Turkish or Turkish Cypriot security, it could unilaterally withdraw many of the approximately 40,000 troops it deploys in northern Cyprus to help lessen Greek Cypriot feelings of insecurity and show them that Turkey is prepared for change. Ankara should also consider trying to break the deadlock with the EU over its accession process by agreeing to open its ports to Greek Cypriot vessels even in the absence of a simultaneous lifting of the EU's ban on direct trade with northern Cyprus, currently a nonnegotiable precondition of Erdogan. Allowing Greek Cypriot ships to use Turkish ports, already agreed to in principle as part of the Additional Protocol to the customs union with the EU, would in no way imply recognition of the Greek Cypriot administration, would benefit the Turkish economy, would eliminate a major roadblock in the Turkish path to EU accession, and would earn Turkey credit with its allies in the EU while putting pressure on the Greek Cypriot side to make reciprocal gestures. Continuing to refuse to move on the ports issue is not accomplishing its stated goal of forcing the EU to trade with Turkish Cypriots, but it does serve as a pretext for Cyprus and some Turkey-skeptic EU members to continue to block Turkey's accession process.

Realistically, even gestures like these and intensified U.S. and EU efforts to promote negotiations may not succeed in producing a political settlement. Greek Cypriots, secure in their status as full members of the European Union, feel that time is on their side and see little reason for compromise. The Cyprus stalemate has endured despite extensive international efforts for over thirty years, and it would be unrealistic to count on it to be broken anytime soon. If there is little the United States and Europe can do in the near term to reach a final settlement, however, they can and should do more to counter the perception among Turks that Turkey has yet again gotten the short end of the stick. If a renewed push to reach a political settlement fails, the United States and EU should do more to implement their promises to lessen the Turkish Cypriots' isolation.

The EU operates under significant constraints in what it can do to facilitate Turkey's membership because of the Cypriot veto power, but it can and should push to disburse the funds it has allocated for northern Cyprus, press Nicosia to allow direct trade with northern Cyprus, open up European sporting and cultural events to Turkish Cypriot participants, and expand diplomatic contacts between member states and elected Turkish Cypriot officials. The United States is less constrained than the EU and should therefore go even further. Washington should increase the amount of financial assistance (so far around $30 million) it has allocated to assist Turkish Cypriot businesses in the banking, agriculture, and tourism sectors; encourage expanded congressional and private-sector contacts with northern Cyprus; and normalize the periodic meetings the U.S. secretary of state has held with the Turkish Cypriot president since 2005. The United States should not recognize northern Cyprus as an independent state, but it should remind Greek Cypriots intent on isolating it that over time as prospects for reunification will recede, recognition by other states may well take place, de facto partition and Turkish Cypriot integration with Turkey will continue, and insecurity will prevail—all to the detriment of everyone involved. Such measures would show Turks that they still have friends in the West and also could help convince Greek Cypriots to come back to the table to negotiate the sort of political settlement that remains the preferable option.

* * *

The agenda spelled out in this book is an ambitious one that clearly requires difficult tradeoffs and political risk. But given the stakes involved, leaders in the United States and Europe should really think carefully about what they can do now to revive the fading partnership with Turkey before it is too late. None of these challenges is impossible. The benefits of a renewed partnership with Turkey would be enormous for all sides. The next U.S. president should not have to debate "who lost Turkey" but instead should do everything possible to avoid that question even being posed.

Afterword:
Turkey's Western Trajectory

SOLI OZEL

THE THEME OF Philip Gordon and Omer Taspinar's *Winning Turkey* is that country's relations with the West. In a carefully delineated argument they present their case as to why Turkey is important for the West and propose (five policy) steps for the United States to take that will secure Turkey's commitment to the Western alliance while consolidating its democracy. One of their persistent themes is that Turkey's Western orientation should not be taken for granted, and can be most safely secured if sustained by a domestic liberal democratic order. In other words, a *"bon pour l'orient"* type of democracy—one exhibiting features that would be rejected in a mature Western democracy—that was acceptable during the cold war is no longer a viable option. Furthermore, they draw attention to dynamics within Turkey that make it less than certain that Turkey wishes to remain unquestioningly on the path of Westernization. At the very least, they point out, the depth of resentment against the West—partly as a result of American policies (notably the Iraq War) and partly as a result of European snubs—makes the task of selling this Western orientation to the broader Turkish public more difficult.

In strategic terms as well, whereas during the cold war membership in the Western security system was taken for granted, the post–cold war period gradually led to a search for new orientations on the part of some critical actors. Undoubtedly for some, particularly in Islamist circles, the desire to engage with the larger Muslim world and the Middle East was strong. The initiative by the Islamist prime minister Necmeddin Erbakan to form an economic club of leading Muslim countries, the D-8, in 1997 was one manifestation of that desire. Another alternative, the Eurasian perspective proposed by Turkish secularist nationalists and identified by the authors, was meant to move Turkey away from its Western alliance system. The rationale behind such searches for foreign policy alternatives was the perception or conviction that Turkey's interests and those of its erstwhile allies were no longer in sync.

In fact, so the secularist nationalists' argument went, Turkey's and Western democracies' interests were often at odds with one another. The proof of such a point of view was the Iraq War, when the clash of interests between Washington and Ankara became painfully obvious. For these nationalists, the United States violated Turkey's most sacredly held national interest and seemed to encourage the founding of a Kurdish state. The domestic political vision that complemented this so-called Eurasian alternative, which led in some circles to deep admiration for Vladimir Putin and Putinism, was an authoritarian-secularist Turkey. The secularist nationalists also defended closer strategic cooperation with Iran, although the desire of staunch secularists to harmonize policies with Islamist Iran was certainly an anomaly.

As the authors state, it is impossible to separate Turkey's foreign policy choices from its domestic issues, the legacy of its history, the power struggles within its polity, and the ongoing transformation of Turkish society. The end of the cold war, the refashioning of the Middle Eastern state system, and new power balances in the Persian Gulf and the Caucasus undoubtedly create for Turkey new strategic opportunities. The relative stability of Turkey's politics and the appeal of its economic success and dynamism prepare the geopolitical structural conditions for the rise of neo-Ottomanist designs in foreign policy. But so do the urbanization of Turkey, the rise of a new, more conservative and religious provincial business class, and the coming of age of a more Islamically oriented counter-elite.

Just this combination alone, at a time when debates abound concerning the nature of Islam as a religion and its compatibility with democracy or secularism, has put Turkey in the spotlight of Western political analysis and foreign policy discussions. As a result, in the years since 2003 arguably more has been written on Turkey—its politics, its strategic importance in the post–cold war and post–September 11 world, and the Turkish experiment in nation building itself—than in the previous fifty.

Since the Turkish military issued its so-called e-memorandum on April 27, 2007, to block the election of then Foreign Minister Abdullah Gul as president, news from Turkey has frequently occupied the front pages and the editorial columns of major newspapers around the world. Recently two court cases—one concerning the closure of the ruling Justice and Development Party (AKP) and the other, the so-called Ergenekon case, concerning the elimination of rogue elements within the security apparatuses of the Turkish state as well as the exposure of former military commanders for having tried to stage coups in 2003 and 2004—have drawn much attention. For most domestic and foreign observers, it was inconceivable that the ruling party of a democracy would be charged with subverting the regime it governed, let alone be guilty of such subversion. The case and the debates surrounding it polarized public opinion and finally came to a happy ending on July 30, when the Constitutional Court found the AKP guilty as charged but not so guilty as to deserve closure. With this sublimely if shamefully political decision the court kept the AKP in place, put it on probation, and gave the country a respite from the poisonous atmosphere.

The Ergenekon case, too, exposed the deep fissures in the country. Some segments of the population and dominant newspapers of the mainstream press approached the case with suspicion. They questioned the motives of the prosecutor and linked the progress of the Ergenekon case to the closure case, suggesting implicitly or explicitly that the government's ulterior motive in pursuing this case was to move against its detractors who might be implicated. In an environment where the judicial processes are overpoliticized, such a supposition may be considered justified. However, the facts unearthed by the voluminous if flawed indictment—some 2,500 pages and hundreds of thousands of documents of evidence—make it necessary to take the case seriously.

In view of the enthusiasm generated by the July 22, 2007, election results both domestically and abroad, it is hard to believe how rapid the deterioration of Turkey's political fortunes was. How did the euphoria of Election Day, when the electorate sent a strong message to the military to keep out of civilian politics and boosted the power of a conservative party with Islamist roots, segue into the state of affairs of summer 2008? Will the Constitutional Court's decision just lead to a temporary lull in hostilities, or will the country's political actors use the occasion to finally deal with the fundamental problems of the Turkish Republic?

On the one hand, Turkey's established political system is sclerotic, as evidenced by its current distribution of institutional power and its approach to the role of Islam in politics (namely, it should have either no role or a subservient one) and to the

Kurdish question. The authors identify these as two of the three main pillars of Kemalism, namely "radical secularism" and "assimilationist nationalism." Turkey seems to be unable to devise new ways and methods of thinking within the existing paradigm so as to rise to the challenges that a more market-oriented, socially mobile, urbanized—if not yet urbane and politically transformed—Turkey faces in the post–cold war era. This in turn leads the established order's custodians to revert to authoritarian methods and in some cases to vilification of just that "West" of which the Turkish Republic at its foundation explicitly aspired to be an equal member. This drive for Westernization is the third main pillar of Kemalism. Secularist nationalists resent Western pressures for liberal democratization as much because of the power shift such a course entails as because of their ideological commitment to a peculiarly fashioned understanding of secularism delineated in this book.

On the other hand, the challengers of the established order (represented in this instance by the AKP) lack the comprehensive vision, the imagination, and the cadres that are necessary to transform the system along liberal democratic lines and to consolidate the rule of law. It may well be unfair to expect the AKP, a self-styled conservative party, to go beyond its own agenda, customs, and worldview and push for a more radical liberalization and democratization of Turkey's political landscape. Thus, the fact remains that the agents of a possible new order are incapable of taking over from a corroded old system, much less of substantively transforming it. Together, these two groups of political agents—the establishment and its challengers—condemn a dynamic, vibrant, aspiring nation to stasis, confusion, and crisis. The malaise thus engendered manifests itself in a multidimensional polarization, and the poles are defined in the language of the politics of identity. This is not simply a matter of Turkey's aligning its foreign policy with the West—it goes further and deeper than that.

The Litigation against the AKP

To assess the full implications of Turkey's political and constitutional crisis it may be useful to review the mechanics and the facts of the process that began to unfold in spring 2008. On March 31, 2008, the Constitutional Court agreed to consider the case to close down the ruling AKP and ban seventy-one of its active and retired politicians from politics. The list of politicians to be banned included the sitting president of the Republic, Abdullah Gul, and Prime Minister Recep Tayyip Erdogan. There is little doubt in the minds of most observers that the 162-page indictment prepared by the prosecutor general of the High Court of Appeals was more a political document than a legal one.

Along with some legally dubious arguments, the indictment documented instances since 2003 when the listed personalities said or did things that the prosecutor deemed to be in violation of the principle of secularism. The text also included commentary by the prosecutor that saw the alleged efforts by the AKP to Islamize Turkey as an extension, if not the direct outcome, of Great Power strategies.

Following the AKP's election win in July 2007—prior to the launch of the court case—Turkey's prospects looked very different. These elections were held earlier than scheduled because the military intervened in the process of electing the AKP's foreign minister, Abdullah Gul, as Turkey's new president. Turkish democracy proved its maturity and the AKP won a landslide victory in the parliamentary elections. The AKP then had the chance to overhaul Turkey's system by drafting a new, more democratic constitution. It had a mandate to continue with the EU reform process that it had basically ignored for the previous two and a half years. Instead, after an initial attempt in September–October 2007 to present a new constitution drafted by a panel of experts it had commissioned, the AKP acted as if it did not wish to spend much political capital on the arduous EU reform process. With its sights fixed on the municipal elections of 2009, the party must have concluded that the EU as a cause had no domestic political payback. Nor did the party show much interest in seeking a broad consensus for its major initiatives. The most daring AKP move was changing two articles of the constitution with the help of the ultranationalist Nationalist Action Party (Milliyetci Hareket Partisi—MHP) to allow headscarf-wearing students to attend classes at the university.

In early June the Constitutional Court ruled that the amendments to the constitution were themselves unconstitutional and declared these null and void and effectively made the headscarf ban permanent.

After hesitating between different options that ranged from a defiant set of amendments to the constitution that would make party closing much more difficult to doing nothing at all, the AKP decided just to follow the procedure. It presented its defense and asked for no extra time, an indication that it wanted the matter to be over as soon as possible and wanted to have enough time to regroup if the decision was for the party to be banned.

During this period, though, the AKP made no moves to reach out to the significant segment of the population that is concerned about the rising profile of religion in public life but does not share the innate antagonism of AKP's fierce secularist opponents. It also has not shown the public the way out of the crisis.

The Kurdish nationalist Democratic Society Party (Demokratik Toplum Partisi—DTP) has also been challenged with possible closure by the court. If both the AKP and DTP were to be closed down, the two parties that together have received about 85 percent of the votes in Turkey's predominantly Kurdish southeast would have been driven out of politics. Such an eventuality could have dire consequences for Turkey's national cohesion: it would further alienate Turkey's Kurdish population, could play into the hands of the Kurdish Workers' Party (Partiya Karkeren Kurdistan—PKK), and might rekindle widespread terrorism in the region and elsewhere. This was precisely the line of argument AKP strategists presented both to the public and to state elites. An unidentified senior member of the AKP government (widely believed to be the former justice minister and current deputy prime minister, Cemil Cicek) noted in a conversation with the journalist Fikret Bila of *Milliyet*, "While Turkish politics is immersed in this fight, what will happen when both sides suddenly realize that they can no longer go to the southeast? . . . [If the AKP is closed down], political ties to the southeast will have all been cut except for the [pro-PKK] DTP." There are intricate relations between developments in Turkey concerning the Kurdish issue and PKK terrorism and the political situation in northern Iraq as well as Turkey's relations with the region. Given this context, the repercussions of closing the AKP would potentially not be confined to Turkey.

For understandable reasons, the unfolding stories and particularly the closure case elicited a strong response from the European Union, which is holding accession negotiations with Turkey. Enlargement Commissioner Olli Rehn immediately criticized the indictment and the propensity to close down political parties. The idea of suspending accession negotiations with Turkey (a notion that was never realistic but enjoyed considerable support among Turkey bashers within the EU) entered circulation. The long-scheduled visit to Turkey of the head of the European Commission, Jose Manuel Barroso, took place in this environment. In his contacts and speeches Barroso reiterated the EU's commitment to negotiation for Turkey's full membership, suggested a preference for a more liberal interpretation of secularism, and expressed his view that the headscarf issue is a matter of personal choice and not a symbol of an existential threat to the secularism of the Republic.

The American response to the court case was more subdued. Officials at first voiced their wish that both Turkey's secularism and its democracy be safeguarded, an almost neutral and therefore inadequate position vis-à-vis the two sides of the ongoing political struggle. This was partially a function of the desire not to jeopardize the recent improvements in Turkish-U.S. relations (which have suffered because of the Iraq War) resulting from the United States' giving Turkey critical help in its fight against PKK camps and Kurdish fighters in northern Iraq. Washington may have wished to avoid antagonizing the military by taking too strong a position against the prosecution of the case, since it believes, rightly, that it could not determine its outcome. The position could even be a function, as many pundits in Turkey claimed, of the divisions within the U.S. administration concerning the AKP and the nature of that party's rule and intentions. Still, the concerns of the U.S. government about the effects of the case and the possible closure of the AKP on Cyprus and on relations with Iraqi Kurds and with Armenia were voiced by Ambassador Ross Wilson when he met with AKP deputies. In retrospect it is becoming evident as well that the United States may have exerted subtle but effective pressure on authorities by making its displeasure with the idea of closure known.

The Constitutional Court was thus put in the unenviable position of becoming the final arbiter of Turkey's politics and the ultimate custodian of its secularism—burdened with the task of blocking a steamroller AKP that Turkey's other political parties were unable to contain or balance. But this level of politicization of the judiciary in general and the Constitutional Court in particular risked ending in a descent into a regime crisis.

Ultimately the court did not assume this burden partially to preserve the integrity of the institution. Despite the conviction of ten of its members that the ruling AKP was indeed engaged in anti-secular activities, it did not hand down a closure decision, instead simply cutting by half the amount the party received from the treasury. The justices probably took the domestic and international context of their decision into account. Fierce opposition within the country to the case in general, an outright reprimand from the European Union, and belated yet consistent probing from Washington all played their part in determining the outcome.

The Constitutional Court in the end acknowledged the supremacy of the ballot box in a democratic order and refrained from jeopardizing Turkey's relations with its Western democratic allies. Ironically, by making a primarily political decision the court also reinforced the view that in Turkey the legal system is one of the instruments of politics and not an independent, impartial branch of government. Indeed, the court's decision to put the AKP on probation also meant that the conviction of those within the justice system that they are empowered to exercise tutelage over politicians was alive and well. These are habits the country needs to shed as rapidly as possible.

Ultimately the decision was a significant gain for Turkish democracy, despite the shadow cast by the notion of the judiciary's tutelage over politics. It returned the resolution of the country's problems to where they belonged, that is, the political sphere. However the polarization along the secular-religious axis and the broader struggle over the redistribution of power in the polity that were at the roots of the case are still in place, as is the lack of trust that pervades the opposing political camps.

In the wake of the decision that headed off a potentially severe systemic crisis, the first task of all stakeholders ought to be the refashioning of Turkey's political and administrative structures. The many crises the country currently experiences are actually signs of painful, traumatic change. So it is incumbent upon the civilian political actors, mainly the elected representatives in Parliament, to ease this transformation and help build a bona fide democracy.

Turkey Still Looking West

Many Western observers, particularly in the United States, have of late been concerned about Turkey's possible drift away from the West. Some of the more vocal among them hold the AKP and its Islamist roots responsible for such a turn, which would lead to privileged relations with Turkey for Middle Eastern countries, most notably Iran and Syria. As the present volume and the foregoing analysis and observations make clear, however, the character of Turkey's international relations and the nature of its policy choices are such that a simple dichotomous West vs. East approach cannot cover all nuances. The problems of Turkey's sense of political identity and cultural belonging run deep. The cultural and political fault lines of the country—secular-Islamic, Sunni-Alevi (a subgroup of Islam), Turkish-Kurdish—are amassing energy. The continuing irresolution of problems related to these fault lines, the collective inability to reach a consensus toward reformulating the Turkish polity, and managing these tensions within a democratic framework are straining societal relations. Furthermore, basic facts of recent Turkish political history inform us that in such conditions illicit organizations or even some state agencies can engage in provocative actions and contribute further to the polarization in society.

This was in fact precisely what the Ergenekon case brought to the light of day. The case, being heard in the Istanbul Court of Assize, was built against an illicit organization that called itself Ergenekon (from the founding legend of the Turkish nation). The prosecution, after an investigation that lasted for thirteen months, prepared a voluminous indictment against a network of security personnel, business people, mafiosi, journalists, and assorted others who had organized themselves to undertake the overthrow of the civilian government, create conditions for a military coup, abrogate the constitutional order, and engage in terrorist activities. It is becoming evident that the organization—a spinoff from cold war–era extralegal organizations whose raison d'être was to fight the Soviets in case of invasion of a NATO country, but that also engaged in illedgal activities—was responsible for numerous unsolved murders and sensational terrorist activities since 1990 as well.

The indicted—eighty-six individuals so far, including two retired generals—are being charged with, among other things, forming a terrorist organization. It is expected that at least one additional indictment will be prepared against the former commander of the gendarmerie for having attempted to stage two military coups back in 2003 and 2004 while on active duty. These attempts were aborted by the then chief of staff and his immediate subordinates at the general staff. (The story of these attempts is chronicled in the diaries of the former commander of the navy, although he denies that the diaries, published by a now defunct weekly magazine, are his).

All available information suggests that the case is at least partially about the reconstruction of the Turkish military. By now it is clearly understood that two broadly defined camps within the military were fighting it out for ideological dominance within the institution. One is still West-oriented and therefore supportive of the democratic order; the other is more Eurasia-oriented, prone to secular authoritarianism and willing to move Turkey in the direction of Russia. Ergenekon in that sense is a cleaning-up operation. Both the success in aborting the coups in 2003 and 2004 and the generally supportive posture of the current military top brass regarding the Ergenekon arrests and indictments mean that the days of military intervention and rule in Turkey are finally over. Even if the legal case does not go as far as it currently promises, the political significance of the case and its liberating effect on Turkey's civilian politics are to be celebrated.

The domestic political convulsions in Turkey are to a considerable extent also related to the end of the cold war and the strategic disorientation this has generated among policymakers, particularly in the context of the Iraq War. The end of the cold war changed the basic parameters of Turkey's relations with the West. Although Ankara remained committed to the transatlantic alliance, it also felt that its partners did not appreciate Turkey's particular security concerns. In fact, Turkish authorities and the public long suspected that the PKK was being given shelter by European allies and the United States. It also became evident that the commonality of security and strategic interests that existed during the cold war was no longer as easily identifiable. The most dramatic illustration of this was the parliament's refusal to allow the deployment of American troops to open a northern front against Iraq, a decision supported by a majority of the public and a significant section of decisionmaking elites, including the then president of the Republic, Ahmet Necdet Sezer.

The sum of these many issues is that Turkey's domestic politics and foreign policy orientation and preferences are linked in contradictory ways. The traditional Westernizing elites are resentful of the West because of pressures to democratize that in their minds are akin to encouraging both separatism and Islamization.

Democratization of the Turkish political order does indeed mean a profound shift in the balance of power and this process entails loss of power and privilege for those on the losing side. Therefore the most virulent anti-Western positions as well as proposals for a non-Western strategic option nowadays come from some Westernized elites, including retired military officers. The ideological content of the language of that resentment and reaction is either the sanctity of secularism at the expense of democracy or the threat to the territorial integrity of the country.

As Gordon and Taspinar point out, a transformation has taken place such that the AKP and the Islamically inclined forces in the country that were the standard bearers of anti-Westernism have converted into the unlikely and at times reluctant champions of Turkey's Western orientation. Since the general election in July 2007 their lack of commitment to liberal democratic principles and their lethargy about the EU accession process have cost them significant support among people who are not necessarily part of a power bloc but jealously defend their secular lifestyles.

Far more important for Turkey's future than the issue of secularism is the Kurdish problem. The irresolution of that problem and the continuation of PKK terrorism turn the politics of Turkey into a tinderbox. The way the domestic Kurdish problem is handled is closely linked to the way Turkey relates to northern Iraq and the Iraqi Kurds. For some years now the AKP government has wanted to improve relations with Iraqi Kurds and end the awkward situation in which Turkey spoke with all the parties in Iraq except the Kurds. Turkey was the only neighboring country that Iraqi President Talabani did not visit because former President Sezer and the military were opposed to meeting him. The opportunity to change course came when the United States finally took a more straightforward position against the PKK after the organization overplayed its hand by resorting to terrorism following the general elections. The elections clearly demonstrated that public support for terrorism, or at least support for violence, had considerably declined among the Kurds of Turkey.

In light of the support given by the United States to Turkey in its struggle against the PKK, many observers in Turkey also expected the government to finally deliver on its promises to present a major reform package on the Kurdish issue. This has not happened and is unlikely to happen, given the party's current troubles and resistance from within the ranks by conservative-nationalist elements. The government wishes to open more channels of cooperation toward northern Iraq and Iraqi Kurds in order to better isolate the PKK and gain the trust of Turkey's own Kurds, but it is being blocked by the security establishment. Rising PKK terrorism or a spectacular terrorist incident perpetrated by the PKK would rekindle both the anti-Kurdish and the currently subdued anti-American sentiment in the country.

In the wake of the Constitutional Court's decision on closure of the AKP and with the unfolding of the Ergenekon case, one can conclude that the days of military intervention and terror by rogue elements in Turkey are over. The political sphere now has an opportunity to build a truly civilian system where the rule of law is indeed supreme. Turkey's secularism debate, the Kurdish problem, and the general question of minority rights will still take some time to be resolved. It is the contention of Gordon and Taspinar that this can only be accomplished if Turkey consolidates its democracy. The most significant symbol of the will to do this is the rekindling of the EU accession process, which must move forward, at times in spite of actions or words of the EU or some of its members. This is the challenge facing the AKP, which needs to own up to this goal and drop the complacency it has shown over the past three years. In the absence of a viable opposition that pressures the AKP to move in the direction of EU accession, this may be politically inconvenient, inexpedient, and even difficult. But it is the right thing to do. Only when Turkey clearly chooses this path, will there be no need to figure out ways of "winning Turkey."

SOLI OZEL
Istanbul
August 2008

Notes

Chapter One

1. Pew Global Attitudes Project, "Global Economic Gloom—China and India Notable Exceptions," survey results, June 2008. The survey revealed that only 12 percent of Turks had a "favorable view" of the United States, the lowest percentage for any of the twenty-four countries surveyed (http://pewglobal.org/reports/pdf/260.pdf). This was a slight increase from the nine percent of Turks with a favorable view of the United States the previous year, also the lowest ranking among forty-seven countries surveyed (http://pewglobal.org/reports/display.php?ReportID=256).

Chapter Two

1. Turkey has a parliamentary system in which primary executive power rests with the prime minister. However, the 1982 constitution, written under military rule, significantly increased the power of the presidency. The president, who is elected by the parliament, has the right to veto constitutional amendments and to make top nominations for posts in the judiciary and academia, such as the head of the Higher Education Board and the deans of public universities.

2. Interviews in Turkey, September 2007 and June 2008. The citation is from Fareed Zakaria, "Worries about Turkey are 'Fact-Free Paranoia,'" *Newsweek*, May 14, 2007.

3. "Chief Prosecutor of the Court of Appeals Indictment against the AKP" (www.yargitay.gov.tr/media/2797.doc, p. 117).

101

4. Statements the prosecutor considered to be violations of the principle of secularism include the following: "In Turkey, where 99 percent of the population is Muslim, religion is a cement uniting different groups" (p. 29); "A democratic country should provide religious freedom. . . . The headscarf ban is not in tune with liberal principles" (p. 34); "We want to solve the headscarf issue through a consensus with other political parties" (p. 35); "We aim to end all cases of discrimination by creating a general consensus on civil liberties" (p. 45); "My biggest wish is a country where girls wearing a headscarf and those without a headscarf would walk hand in hand" (p. 48); "Devout people, too, have a right to engage in politics in this country" (p. 52); "It is sad that our young female students are barred from education just because of their headscarf" (p. 74); "The authority that can give a final decision [on whether the headscarf is mandated by Islam or not] is the High Council for Religious Matters of the Directorate of Religious Affairs" (p. 83); and "The headscarf ban is against human rights" (p. 91). "Chief Prosecutor of the Court of Appeals Indictment against the AKP" (www.yargitay.gov.tr/media/2797.doc).

5. Figures are per capita at market exchange rates. For 2001 see United States Department of State, Country Profile, Turkey, October 2003. For 2007 see Economist Intelligence Unit, Fact Sheet, Turkey, May 20, 2008.

6. On the *Nokta* report and possible coup, see European Stability Initiative, *Turkey's Dark Side: Party Closures, Conspiracies and the Future of Democracy*, ESI Briefing, Berlin-Istanbul, April 2, 2008.

Chapter Three

1. Kemal Kirisci, "Turkey's Encounter with Europe and Its Attitude toward Greece and Cyprus," abstract and outline prepared for conference "Cyprus's European Accession and the Greece-Turkey Rivalry," Yale University, April 4–6, 2003 (www.yale.edu/eustudies/Cyprus_Conference_Kirisci.pdf).

2. See *Turkish Daily News,* online poll "Which Is Turkey's Best Friend?" July 8, 2006 (www.turkishdailynews.com.tr/poll/test1.php?action=results&poll_id=13).

3. See Pew Global Attitudes Project survey, "Global Economic Gloom" (see note 1 to chapter 1). The percentage of "favorable opinions" of the United States among Turks was 23 percent in 2005, 12 percent in 2006, and 9 percent in 2007.

4. Karl Vick, "In Many Turks' Eyes, U.S. Remains the Enemy," *Washington Post,* April 10, 2005; Sixteen-Nation Pew Global Attitudes Project, "U.S. Image Up Slightly, but Still Negative," survey, released June 23, 2005; according to the German Marshall Fund of the United States, *Transatlantic Trends: Key Findings 2007* (Washington: 2007), 77 percent of Turks found the U.S. administration's global leadership to be "undesirable."

5. The others were Palestinian Territories, 48 percent; Egypt, 39 percent; Lebanon, 38 percent; Kuwait, 26 percent; Jordan, 25 percent; Morocco, 17 percent; Israel, 4 percent (see note 1 to chapter 1).

6. See Carol Migdalovitz, "Iraq: Turkey, the Deployment of U.S. Forces, and Related Issues," Congressional Research Service Report (Washington: May 2, 2003).

7. Dexter Filkins, "Turkish Deputies Refuse to Accept American Troops," *New York Times*, March 2, 2003.

8. Wolfowitz quote: interview with CNN Turk, May 6, 2003 (www.defense link.mil/transcripts/2003/tr20030506-depsecdef0156.html).

9. Interview with George Stephanopolous, "This Week with George Stephanopolous," March 20, 2005, ABC News transcript.

10. Dexter Filkins with Douglas Jehl, "Turkey Says U.S. Has Agreed to Free 11 Soldiers Suspected in Plot to Kill Kurdish Aide," *New York Times*, July 7, 2003, p. A6; Nicholas Birch, "Detention Strains Already Tense US-Turkey Relations," *Christian Science Monitor*, July 15, 2003; James C. Helicke, "U.S. General Seeks to Ease Tensions with Turkey Following the Detention of 11 Turkish Soldiers," AP, July 8, 2003.

11. Cited in Amberin Zaman, "Turkey Drifts Further from U.S.," *Los Angeles Times*, December 14, 2004.

12. Ibid.

13. Ibid.

14. "Remarks by Ambassador Ross Wilson Concerning the Visit by Hamas Leaders to Turkey," Ankara, February 16, 2006 (http://turkey.usembassy.gov/amb_021606.html).

15. Cited in Umit Enginsoy and Burak Egebekdil, "Hamas Chief's Visit Tests Turk-U.S. Ties," *Defense News*, February 27, 2006.

16. Henri J. Barkey, "Two Faced on Terrorism," *Los Angeles Times*, March 11, 2006.

17. "Turkish PM Condemns 'New Culture of Violence' in Mideast," Agence France-Presse, July 31, 2006.

18. Quentin Peel, "Anti-West Backlash Is Gathering Pace, Warns Turkish Minister," *Financial Times*, July 20, 2006.

19. Authors' interviews with AKP officials, Ankara, May 2007.

20. Sebnem Arsu, "Turk Warns Against House Genocide Motion," *New York Times*, October 15, 2007.

21. White House, Office of the Press Secretary, "Press Conference by the President," October 17, 2007.

22. U.S. State Department, "Press Availability with Foreign Minister Ali Babacan," press release, November 2, 2007; White House, Office of the Press Secretary, "President Bush and Prime Minister Erdogan Discuss Global War on Terror," press release, November 5, 2007.

23. Ellen Knickmeyer and Joshua Partlow, "Turkish Warplanes Again Cross Border to Bomb in N. Iraq: Strike against Rebel Kurds Is at Least 3rd in 10 Days: White House Urges Restraint," *Washington Post,* December 27, 2007.

24. Gates comment: U.S. Department of Defense, "Media Roundtable with Secretary of Defense Robert Gates, India, February 27, 2008," DefenseLink transcript (www.defenselink.mil/transcripts/transcript.aspx?transcriptid=4161). Odierno: Following an observation that U.S. support for Turkey's intervention "really has helped improve relations between the United States, Turkey, and the government of Iraq," Odierno said, "I also believe that the long-term solution in northern Iraq is not a military one. And so–but obviously there's pressures that have to be put on them, so we can start to talk and have negotiations with these terrorist elements." See "Special Defense Department briefing with Lieutenant General Ray Odierno," March 4, 2008 (www.globalsecurity.org/military/library/news/2008/03/mil-080304-dod01.htm).

25. See Admiral William Fallon, Testimony before the House Armed Services Committee, March 5, 2008.

Chapter Four

1. "Turkey and Europe: Just Not Our Sort," *The Economist,* March 15, 1997.

2. "Germany Angrily Rejects Ankara's Accusations of Lebensraum Policy," Associated Press, March 6, 1998.

3. The summit declaration stated that "Turkey is a candidate State destined to join the Union on the basis of the same criteria as applied to the other candidate States." See European Council, Millennium Declaration, paragraph 12 (www.europarl.europa.eu/summits/hel1_en.htm).

4. Eurobarometer 64: Public Opinion in the EU, June 2006 (http://ec.europa.eu/public_opinion/archives/eb/eb64/eb64_en.htm).

5. See European Council, "Negotiating Framework: Principles Governing the Negotiations," paragraph 2 (http://ec.europa.eu/enlargement/pdf/st20002_05_tr_framedoc_en.pdf).

6. Sixty-five percent of Turkish Cypriots supported the Annan Plan, but 76 percent of Greek Cypriots rejected it. For a good discussion, see International Crisis Group, *Cyprus: Reversing the Drift to Partition*, Europe Report 190, January 10, 2008, p. 4 (executive summary available at www.crisisgroup.org/home/index.cfm?id=5255&l=1).

7. See European Union, General Affairs Council, "Turkish Cypriot Community," April 26, 2004 (http://ec.europa.eu/enlargement/turkish_cypriot_community/index_en.htm; also, Judy Dempsey, "Envoys Meet to Decide Reward for Turkish Cypriots," *Financial Times,* April 27, 2004.

8. For details on the status of EU regulations regarding aid for and trade with the Turkish Cypriot community, see EU Commission, "Turkish Cypriot Community" (http://ec.europa.eu/enlargement/turkish_cypriot_community/index_en.htm).

9. See Elaine Sciolino, "Sarkozy Outlines Foreign Policy," *International Herald Tribune*, February 28, 2007; Nicolas Sarkozy, *Testimony: France, Europe and the World in the Twenty-First Century* (New York: HarperCollins, 2007), p. 189.

10. "Sarkozy Opposes Turkish Entry into EU, Vows Referendum," Agence France-Presse, April 24, 2008.

11. German Marshall Fund of the United States, *Transatlantic Trends: Key Findings, 2007* (Washington: 2007).

12. Eurobarometer 68: Public Opinion in the EU, December 2007 (http://ec.europa.eu/public_opinion/archives/eb/eb68/eb68_en.htm).

Chapter Five

1. See Graham E. Fuller, *The New Turkish Republic* (Washington: U.S. Institute of Peace Press, 2008); F. Stephen Larrabee, "Turkey Rediscovers the Middle East," *Foreign Affairs*, July–August 2007.

2. See Ahmet Davutoglu, *Stratejik Derinlik: Türkiye'nin Uluslararasý Konumu* [Strategic depth: Turkey's international position] (Istanbul: Küre, 2003).

3. See Ahmet Davutoglu, "Turkey's Foreign Policy Vision: An Assessment of 2007," *Insight Turkey*, vol. 10, no. 1 (2008), pp. 77–96.

4. General (Ret.) Tuncer Kilinc, "Turkey Should Leave NATO," speech given before the Kemalist Thought Association, May 30, 2007 (www.turkishweekly.net/news.php?id=45366). Kilinc is a former general secretary of the Turkish National Security Council.

5. Fiona Hill and Omer Taspinar, "Turkey and Russia: Axis of the Excluded?" *Survival* (Spring 2006), pp. 81–92.

6. See Gareth Jenkins, "Turkey and Iran Expected to Boost Security Cooperation," *Eurasia Daily Monitor*, April 14, 2008.

7. See "US Looking to Form 'Kurdish State,'" *Iran Daily*, April 5, 2006.

8. "Week in Review: Turkey Signs Unexpected Deal with Iran," *Turkish Daily News*, July 21, 2007.

9. "Iran, Turkey to Discuss Gas Project," *Turkish Daily News*, May 5, 2008.

10. "Turkish Minister, Chinese Official Discuss Trade Development," Anatolia News Agency, August 30, 2007.

11. Larrabee, "Turkey Rediscovers the Middle East."

12. Sevim Songun, "Regional Tourism Fair Grows Two-fold," *Turkish Daily News*, February 16, 2008.

13. Yigal Schleifer, "Turkey Aims for Clout as Regional Mediator," *Christian Science Monitor,* May 6, 2008.

14. Ethan Bronner, "Israel and Syria Announce Talks on Peace Treaty," *New York Times,* May 22, 2008.

15. Kilinc, the retired general who called for Turkey to leave NATO, has also said that Turkey should "protect its secular state and territorial integrity against Western efforts to promote moderate Islam and Kurdish independence." See Kilinc, "Turkey Should Leave NATO." Another retired officer, General Dogan Gures, Turkish General Staff chief of staff from 1990 to 1994, claimed, "The U.S. also wants [to divide Turkey]. They have prepared maps accordingly. Dick Cheney wants this too. He said, 'When you go from west to east our only friends are the Kurds.'" Quoted in Gareth Jenkins, "Former Turkish Commanders Discuss Costs and Benefits of Cross Border Operations against the PKK," *Eurasian Daily Monitor,* November 7, 2007.

Chapter Six

1. Karen DeYoung, "Turkey Pulls U.S. into Decision on Kurds; Ankara Postpones Reaction to Iraq-based Militants until after Meeting with Bush," *Washington Post,* October 27, 2007.

2. Ibid.

3. Amberin Zaman, "Turkey Passes More Reforms in Quest for EU Membership," *Los Angeles Times,* June 20, 2003.

4. Amberin Zaman, "Leader Regrets Turkish Stance toward Kurds," *Los Angeles Times,* August 13, 2005.

5. Gareth Jenkins, "AKP Condemns Judicial Attempts to Close Kurdish Party," *Eurasia Daily Monitor,* November 19, 2007.

6. See "Turkish PM Mulling Amnesty for Kurdish Rebels," Agence France-Presse, December 9, 2007.

7. See Fikrent Bila, *Komutanlar Cephesi* [Generals' front] (Istanbul: Detay Yayinlari, 2007).

8. Buyukanit cited in Burak Akinci, "Military Action No Answer to Turkey's Kurdish Question: Analysts," Agence France-Presse, December 19, 2007.

9. See Henri Barkey, "Kurdistandoff," *National Interest,* July–August 2007, pp. 51–56.

10. Assistant Secretary of State Daniel Fried, quoted in Paul Taylor, "US Urges Turkey to Heed Constitution, Democracy," Reuters, April 28, 2007.

11. U.S. State Department, "Secretary Rice and Deputy Secretary Kimmitt hold a news briefing en route to Sharm el-Sheikh, Egypt," press release, May 1, 2007.

12. "Rehn Warns Turkey EU Bid May Be at Stake If AK Party Is Shut Down," *Today's Zaman,* March 31, 2008 (www.todayszaman.com/tz-web/detaylar.do?

load=detay&link=137703); see also "Secular and Antidemocratic; in Turkey, Another Attempt to Reverse the Elections Won by Moderate Islamists," editorial, *Washington Post*, May 2, 2008.

13. See Henri J. Barkey and Yasemin Congar, "Deciphering Turkey's Elections: The Making of a Revolution," *World Policy Journal*, Fall 2007, p. 64.

14. Katinka Barysch, "More Than Just a Debate about the Headscarf," *Financial Times*, November 7, 2007. See also the good discussion of Turkish constitutional reform in European Stability Initiative, *Turkey's Dark Side: Party Closures, Conspiracies and the Future of Democracy*, ESI Briefing, Berlin-Istanbul, April 2, 2008.

15. C. Onur Ant, "Turkey's Parliament Softens Law Restricting Free Speech," Associated Press, April 30, 2008.

16. See "President Says Penal Code Article Damages Turkey's Image," Anatolian News Agency, November 7, 2007.

17. The Minsk Group was created in 1992 by the Conference on Security and Cooperation in Europe (now the Organization for Security and Cooperation in Europe, OSCE).

18. See International Crisis Group, "Nagorno-Karabakh: Risking War," Europe Report 187, November 14, 2007 ("Executive Summary and Recommendations" available at www.crisisgroup.org/home/index.cfm?id=5157).

19. Responding to pressure from the more than 400,000 French residents of Armenian origin, in fall 2006 the French parliament went so far as to vote to criminalize denial of Armenian genocide. The bill failed to win presidential approval and did not became law, but even so it set off a firestorm in Turkey. See Philip H. Gordon and Omer Taspinar, "Why France Shouldn't Legislate Turkey's Past," *New Republic* online edition, October 30, 2006 (www.brookings.edu/opinions/2006/1030turkey_gordon.aspx).

20. "Turkish Speaker Critical of Justice Minister's Stance on Armenian Conflict," *Hurriyet*, May 27, 2005.

21. See "A Glimmer of Hope, with Ice Cream: Cyprus," *The Economist*, April 26, 2008.

22. The mutual benefits of a Cyprus solution are spelled out in International Crisis Group, *Cyprus: Reversing the Drift to Partition*, Europe Report 190, January 10, 2008, p. 4 (executive summary available at www.crisisgroup.org/home/index.cfm?id=5255&I=1).

Index

Afghanistan, U.S. action in, 29
AKP (Justice and Development
    Party): anti-U.S. views of, 49;
    Constitutional Court ruling
    against closure of, 87–88;
    creation of, 20; on Cyprus issue,
    46–47; division from secularist
    establishment, 5; election victory
    in July 2007, 9–10, 23, 90; EU
    accession views of, 43, 99–100;
    indictment against, 10–11, 68, 87,
    90–94, 99; and Islamization
    agenda, 3, 22–23, 69; nomination
    of Gul for president, 7; philoso-
    phy of, 4, 20–21, 89; possible
    coup to overthrow current
    regime of, 59–60; on support for
    U.S. military invasion of Iraq, 31;
    in 2002 parliamentary elections,
    43; U.S. view of, 35
American Jewish Committee, 33–34
Amnesty laws, 65
"Anatolian tigers," 20, 71
Annan Plan (UN-sponsored, 2004),
    22, 46, 80–81

Anti-Americanism/anti-
    Westernism, 2, 5, 23–24, 49–50,
    98. *See also* European Union; U.S.
    relationship with Turkey
Anti-communism, 15–17
Anti-Semitism, 33
Armenian relations and Armenian
    genocide, 2, 13, 76–80; U.S.
    recognition of Armenian
    genocide, 35, 76, 78
Arms sales to Turkey, 27, 28
Article 301 on speech restrictions,
    71–72, 78,
Asad, Bashar al-, 58
Asad, Hafez al-, 58
Assimilationist nationalism, 13, 89
Ataturk (Mustafa Kemal), 11–12,
    14, 39

Barkey, Henri, 34, 66
Barruso, Jose Manuel, 92–93
Bila, Fikret, 66, 92
Black Sea Economic Cooperation
    (BSEC), 53
Blue Stream gas pipeline, 54

Union, 47; and Cyprus question, 22; and EU membership, 20; imprisonment of, 19; on insurgents in Iraq, 33; and Islamization agenda, 22–23, 69–70; on Israel, 50; on Kurdish relations, 64, 65; litigation to ban, 90; political campaigning of, 9; public opinion of, 3, 20–21; and Russian relations, 53; on support for U.S. military invasion of Iraq, 31; as target of AKP indictment, 11; U.S. view of, 35

Ergenekon case, 87–88, 96–97, 99

Ethnic lobbies in U.S., 27–28

Eurasian alternatives for Turkey, 49–60, 86

European Security and Defense Policy (ESDP), 74

European Union: on Armenian genocide, 78; Customs Union with, 41, 47, 57, 74, 82; and Cyprus issue, 80–84; on indictment of Turkish political parties, 92, 93; Lisbon Treaty ratification, 73; Rapid Reaction Force, 74; rejection of proposed constitution of, 44–45; sympathetic view toward Kurds, 18; Turkish anti-EU sentiment, 34, 48; Turkish relations with, 38–48

European Union accession: AKP view on, 43, 99–100; "Copenhagen Criteria" for, 43–44; Helsinki Summit (1999) position on, 42, 43; Luxembourg Summit (1997) position on, 41; negatives from EU perspective, 39–40, 44, 56–57, 75; privileged partnership instead of full membership, 45, 48, 73; progress toward in 1998–99, 42–43; recommen-

dations on, 74–76, 99–100; stall in process, 38, 44–48, 73; suspension possibility due to AKP indictment, 92, 93; symbolism of to Turks, 39, 40; Turkey's attempts to join, 2, 9, 18, 20, 22, 24; and Turkish military coup possibility, 68–69; Turks' reluctance toward, 48, 73, 98; U.S. support for, 28, 29, 39, 42–43

Fallon, William, 37

Fez, 15

Foreign Affairs Committee (U.S. House), 35

Foreign policy of Turkey, 50–51, 59–60. *See also specific countries*

France: on Armenia and Nagorno-Karabakh, 77, 78; on EU accession of Turkey, 45, 48; as model for Turkish democracy, 12, 13; refusal to approve proposed EU constitution, 44

Franks, Tommy, 31–32

Freedom of speech, 71–72. *See also* Human rights

Gas. *See* Oil and gas

Gates, Robert, 37

Generals' Front (Bila), 66

Genocide. *See* Armenian relations and Armenian genocide

Geographic location of Turkey, 5

Germany, 41–42, 45, 48

Gordon, Philip, 85, 99

Greece-Turkey relations, 42. *See also* Cyprus issue

Gul, Abdullah: on Article 301 speech restrictions, 72; elected as president (August 2007), 10, 23, 90; on Kurdish relations, 64; litigation to ban, 90; military

Lagendijk, Joost, 71
Language, 14, 15, 44, 65–66
Lebanon and Hezbollah, 34, 50, 58
"Lebensraum" policy of Kohl government, 41
Legal system, 14, 21, 44. *See also* Indictment against AKP
Lisbon Treaty ratification, 73
Luxembourg Summit (1997), 41

Marshall Plan, 16
Menderes, Adnan, 16, 27
Merkel, Angela, 42, 48
Meshaal, Khaled, 33
Metal Storm (Turna and Ucar), 26
Middle class, 20, 43, 70–71
Middle East policies: Turkish role in, 50; Turkish view of U.S. policies, 26. *See also specific countries*
Military (Turkish): in cold war, 15–16, 27; coup attempts in 2003 and 2004, 87, 96; coup of 1997 against Welfare Party, 19, 59; coup possibility in 2007, 7, 8–9, 68; coup possibility in future, 59–60; coups by (1960, 1971, and 1980), 16, 27; and Ergenekon case, 96–97; on Islamization agenda of AKP, 23; Israeli cooperation agreement with, 57–58; modernization of, 14; on PKK situation, 65–66; size of, 50
Military (U.S.): cold war bases in Turkey, 27; detaining Turkish special forces in Iraq, 32; seeking to stage Iraq War from Turkey, 30–32, 97
Minsk Group, 77
Mixon, Benjamin R., 62
Muslim Brotherhood, 70

Nagorno-Karabakh, 77–78
Nationalism, 3, 4, 49; assimilationist variant of, 13, 89
Nationalist Action Party (MHP), 10, 91
National Security Council (Turkey), 22, 44
NATO, 15, 16, 27, 40, 47; Georgia's membership in, 53; International Security and Assistance Force (ISAF), 30; size of Turkish force in, 50
Neo-Ottomanism, 51
Nokta on division over Cyprus issue, 22

Ocalan, Abdullah, 29, 42, 58
Odierno, Ray, 37
Oil and gas: access to Caspian Sea and Central Asia, 5, 28, 52, 56; EU-Turkey energy dialogue, 74; exploration jointly with Syria, 58; imports from Iran, 55–56; imports from Russia, 54
Ottoman Empire: European relations of, 38; legacy of, 51; view of religion, 12, 13, 70
Ozal, Turgut, 20, 51
Ozok, Hilmi, 22

Pamuk, Orhan, 71
Party for Free Life in Kurdistan (PJAK), 55
Pelosi, Nancy, 35
Penal Code Article 301. *See* Article 301 on speech restrictions
PKK (Kurdish Workers' Party): amnesty law proposed for, 65; costs of fight with, 18; and possible ban of Kurdish political party, 92; provocative attacks by,

33–34; and Kurdish issue, 35–37, 60, 61–67, 86, 99; maintaining Western orientation of Turkey, 86, 89, 95–100; strain in, 2, 25–37, 28; taking Turkey for granted, 4; Turkish view of, 25–26. *See also* Anti-Americanism/anti-Westernism; Military (U.S.)

Valley of the Wolves (film), 26
Van Gogh, Theo, 45
Virtue Party, 20

War on terrorism, Turkish view of, 26
Water dispute between Turkey and Syria, 57–58
Welfare Party (RP), 11, 18–19, 20, 42

Westernization: advantages of, 5; and Ataturk's policies, 14–15; and cultural gap with rural areas, 15; at end of Ottoman Empire, 38; frustration with, 23–24, 93–97; in preparation for EU accession, 21. *See also* Anti-Americanism/anti-Westernism
Wilson, Ross, 93
Wolfowitz, Paul, 32
Women and dress code, 11, 15. *See also* Headscarf ban
World War I genocide of Armenians. *See* Armenians

Yalcinkaya, Abdurrahman, 10–11
Yilmaz, Mesut, 41
Young Turks, 14, 39

BROOKINGS   The Brookings Institution is a private nonprofit organization devoted to research, education, and publication on important issues of domestic and foreign policy. Its principal purpose is to bring the highest quality independent research and analysis to bear on current and emerging policy problems. The Institution was founded on December 8, 1927, to merge the activities of the Institute for Government Research, founded in 1916, the Institute of Economics, founded in 1922, and the Robert Brookings Graduate School of Economics and Government, founded in 1924. Interpretations or conclusions in Brookings publications should be understood to be solely those of the authors.

Board of Trustees

John L. Thornton
 Chair
Strobe Talbott
 President
Robert J. Abernethy
Liaquat Ahamed
Alan R. Batkin
Richard C. Blum
Geoffrey T. Boisi
Abby Joseph Cohen
Arthur B. Culvahouse Jr.
Alan M. Dachs
Kenneth W. Dam
Steven A. Denning
Vishakha N. Desai
Paul Desmarais Jr.
Thomas E. Donilon

Mario Draghi
Kenneth M. Duberstein
Alfred B. Engelberg
Lawrence K. Fish
Cyrus F. Freidheim Jr.
Bart Friedman
David Friend
Ann M. Fudge
Jeffrey W. Greenberg
Brian L. Greenspun
Glenn Hutchins
Joel Z. Hyatt
Shirley Ann Jackson
Kenneth M. Jacobs
Suzanne Nora Johnson
Philip H. Knight
Harold Hongju Koh

William A. Owens
Frank H. Pearl
John Edward Porter
Edgar Rios
Haim Saban
Sheryl K. Sandberg
Victoria P. Sant
Leonard D. Schaeffer
Lawrence H. Summers
David F. Swensen
Larry D. Thompson
Andrew H. Tisch
Laura D'Andrea Tyson
Antoine W. van Agtmael
Beatrice W. Welters
Daniel Yergin
Daniel B. Zwirn

Honorary Trustees

Leonard Abramson
Elizabeth E. Bailey
Zoë Baird
Rex J. Bates
Louis W. Cabot
James W. Cicconi
A. W. Clausen
William T. Coleman Jr.
D. Ronald Daniel
Robert A. Day
Bruce B. Dayton
Charles W. Duncan Jr.
Walter Y. Elisha
Robert F. Erburu
Henry Louis Gates Jr.
Robert D. Haas
Lee H. Hamilton
William A. Haseltine

Teresa Heinz
F. Warren Hellman
Samuel Hellman
Robert A. Helman
Roy M. Huffington
James A. Johnson
Ann Dibble Jordan
Michael H. Jordan
Vernon E. Jordan Jr.
Breene M. Kerr
Marie L. Knowles
James T. Lynn
Jessica Tuchman Mathews
David O. Maxwell
Donald F. McHenry
Robert S. McNamara
Mary Patterson McPherson
Arjay Miller

Mario M. Morino
Maconda Brown O'Connor
Samuel Pisar
Steven Rattner
J. Woodward Redmond
Charles W. Robinson
James D. Robinson III
Warren B. Rudman
B. Francis Saul II
Ralph S. Saul
Henry B. Schacht
Michael P. Schulhof
Joan E. Spero
Vincent J. Trosino
John C. Whitehead
Stephen M. Wolf
James D. Wolfensohn
Ezra K. Zilkha